GARDEN BIRD FACTS

GARDEN BIRD FACTS

Marcus Schneck

BARNES
&NOBLE
BOOKS
NEW YORK

A QUANTUM BOOK

This edition published by
Barnes & Noble, Inc.,
by arrangement with Quantum Books Ltd
1997 Barnes & Noble Books

ISBN 0-88029-928-2

QUMBDF

M 10 9 8 7 6 5 4 3

This book was produced by
Quantum Books Ltd
6 Blundell Street
London N7 9BH

Senior Editor Sally MacEachern

Editor Eileen Cadman

Art Editor Ashleigh Vinall

Designer Anne Fisher

Illustrators David Ord Kerr (birds), Wayne Ford,
Vana Haggerty, David Kemp

Picture Research Marcus Schneck

Index Connie Tyler

Art Director Moira Clinch

Publishing Director Janet Slingsby

Typeset in Britain by Typestyles (London) Ltd, Harlow, Essex
Manufactured in Singapore by Eray Scan Pte. Ltd
Printed in Singapore by Star Standard Industries Pte. Ltd.

CONTENTS

UNDERSTANDING AND ATTRACTING BIRDS 6

BIRD DIRECTORY 54

UNDERSTANDING AND ATTRACTING BIRDS

When and where did birds originate?

A pigeon-sized reptile-bird that 150 million years ago glided among the forests of what today is Germany was probably the Earth's very first bird. *Archaeopteryx lithographica*, as discoverer Hermann von Meyer named the creature, whose fossil remains were uncovered in 1861 in a quarry near Solenhofen, Germany, was the definitive transitional creature. It had feathers very similar to those of today's birds, but the shape and form of a small, upright reptile with long front legs.

From scales to feathers

The fossil record provides only a few vague clues as to exactly how one group of dinosaurs came to follow the evolutionary path that produced *Archaeopteryx*. An opposable hind claw on its back legs, similar to the apparatus that helps today's birds grasp branches for perching, and unreptilian, long forelegs that probably aided it in clambering about in the trees would seem to tell us that the creature was adapted to life above the forest floor. Feathers, which are made of keratin, the same substance as scales, almost certainly evolved from scales as a means of further enhancing the creature's movements through the trees.

After *Archaeopteryx* the evolution of birds is sketchy at best for 45-50 million years. Only a few different bird-like fossils from that time period have been unearthed. But when a steady fossil record picks up again, birdlife is much more numerous and varied. Some of these fossils can be linked directly to families of birds that exist today.

Controversial fossils

The five complete *Archaeopteryx* skeletons that have been unearthed represent some of the most important fossil support for evolution. They are one of the few true transitional forms that have been discovered.

As such they have been the subject of controversy even to this day. The latest attempt to disprove them as some sort of hoax came in the 1980s. Their authenticity remains intact.

Above: Evolution has taken birdlife in many different directions across the face of the Earth. Among the largest species in the Northern hemisphere is the Canada goose, which pairs for life and is fiercely defensive of its nest, eggs and young.

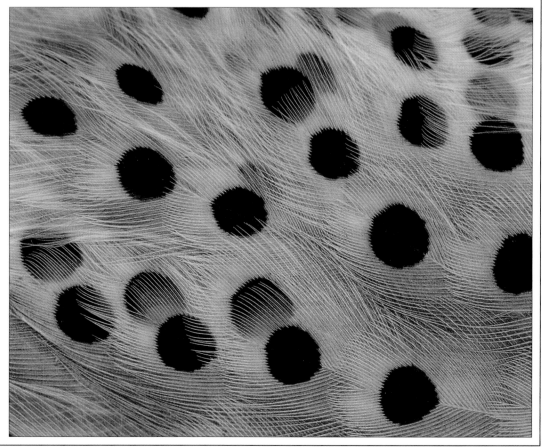

Above: The feather of the first bird-creature, *Archaeopteryx lithographica* is remarkably similar to the feathers of our modern-day birds, such as the example from a yellow-shafted flicker (left). Fossils of the Archaeopteryx (top right), dating to about 150 million years ago were first discovered in 1861 in a quarry in Germany.

Left and above: Although the fossil record seems very clear that the pigeon-sized Archaeopteryx was the precursor to modern birdlife, the skeletal remains of the creature have been at the center of controversy since their discovery more than a century ago. The most recent attempt to discredit them was in the 1980s. It was unsuccessful.

What is "different" about bird physiology?

With few exceptions, birds are "built" to fly. Nearly everything about their skeletal and muscular arrangements signal a creature born to fly.

Bones and muscles

Most of the avian skeleton is hollow and many bones that are individual bones in mammals are fused together in birds. The result is an extremely lightweight creature, with a skeleton that makes up only about 5 percent of its total weight.

The bird's muscles are concentrated around its breast area and at the base of its legs and wings. This creates an aerodynamic shape and a well-focused center of gravity, as well as providing for the power needed in the wings to generate flight.

Digestion

The need for so much power, often in quick bursts, is met by a digestive system geared toward fast and efficient use of all food that's eaten. The bird's stomach is made up of two chambers. The first is equipped with glands that secrete digestive fluids. The second, commonly known as the gizzard, is a muscular apparatus where food is ground to a fine consistency.

Body temperature

Like mammals, birds are warm-blooded. Their body temperature is determined largely by their own, internal heating and cooling system. Birds, however, have generally higher temperatures than mammals which tend to fluctuate more. Unlike humans, but similar to mammals, birds lack sweat glands in the skin. They rely on other means of cooling down, such as feather loss, panting and change of location.

Left: The tiny chipping sparrow looks as if it weighs almost nothing at all. Like most birds, it is even lighter in weight than it looks.

Above: Woodpeckers have a unique physiology, including a skull that contains cushioning tissues to protect the bird brain when it is chiseling into trees.

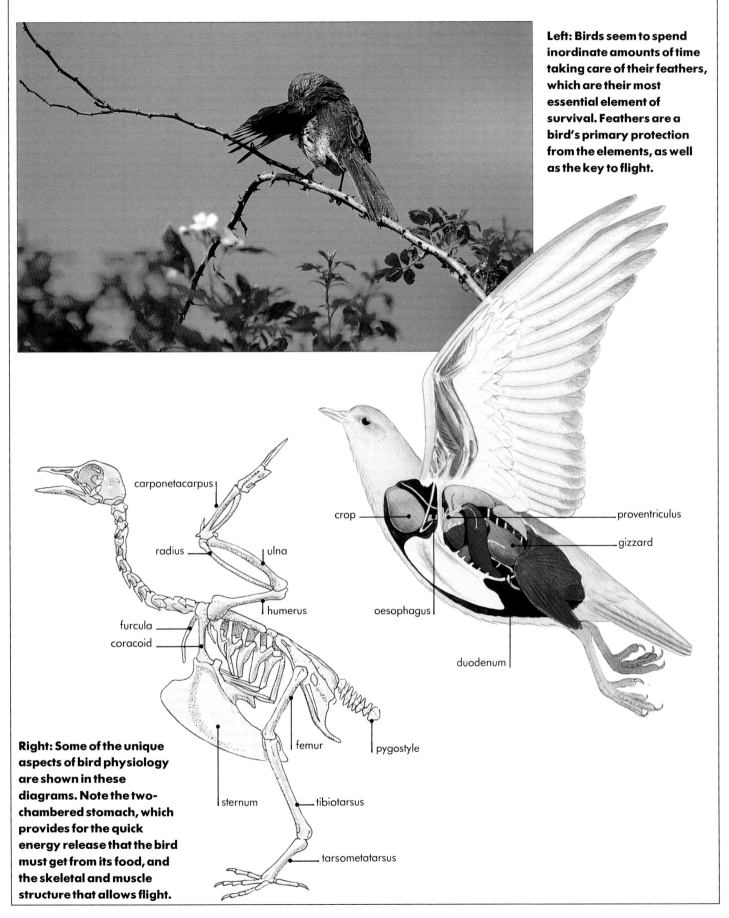

Left: Birds seem to spend inordinate amounts of time taking care of their feathers, which are their most essential element of survival. Feathers are a bird's primary protection from the elements, as well as the key to flight.

carponetacarpus

radius

ulna

humerus

furcula

coracoid

femur

pygostyle

sternum

tibiotarsus

tarsometatarsus

crop

oesophagus

duodenum

proventriculus

gizzard

Right: Some of the unique aspects of bird physiology are shown in these diagrams. Note the two-chambered stomach, which provides for the quick energy release that the bird must get from its food, and the skeletal and muscle structure that allows flight.

How do birds fly?

When lift is greater than weight, the object in question will rise into the air. And, when thrust is greater than drag, that object will move in the direction of the thrust force. These two basic principles explain how birds fly.

They do not, however, explain how birds take advantage of the principles. Wings, of course, are the answer to that question.

Aerodynamic design

The outstretched wing of a bird creates a convex surface, similar to an overturned saucer. Air passing over such a surface moves faster across the top than across the bottom, developing a vacuum above and extra pressure below, in other words, lift. To find the air pressure sufficient enough to get off the ground, birds propel themselves forward in a number of ways, including leaping off a tree or cliff, running across the ground or water surface, and the energy-intensive flapping of the wings. The bird's wing is further adapted to make the most of this lift, and its body is adapted to lessen weight with hollowness of some large bones and a simple, fused skeleton.

The movement of the wing provides the bird's thrust. As the flight muscle (the pectoralis major) contracts it pulls the wing down, but the wing tip also moves forward at the same time. In this motion the primary feathers remain tight together and are bent upward and backward. As the supracoracoideus muscle takes over and contracts it pulls the wing upward. Now the primary feathers separate. The play of these primary feathers with the air acts in the same manner as an airplane's propeller, pulling the bird forward.

Again, the rest of the bird's body is heavily adapted to take full advantage of the thrust created. The avian body is an aerodynamically efficient design. Its spearlike shape cuts through the air. And its outer, rear-directed feathers create a smooth surface that lessens resistance to the air.

Above: Every aspect of a bird's life is affected in one way or another by its ability to fly, with the exception of the few flightless species that survive today.

	wing direction
	wind direction
	lift and thrust

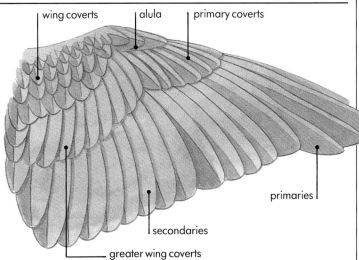

wing coverts | alula | primary coverts

primaries

secondaries

greater wing coverts

Above and below: A combination of factors allow birds to fly; specialized muscles, the feathers that **are unique to birds, and special skeletal structures, that include hollow and fused bones.**

Above: Canada geese are considered among the champion flyers of the bird world because of their legendary fall and spring migrations. However, many smaller birds make even greater migration flights.

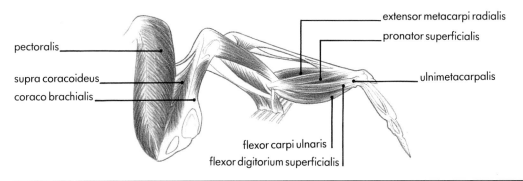

pectoralis

supra coracoideus

coraco brachialis

extensor metacarpi radialis

pronator superficialis

ulnimetacarpalis

flexor carpi ulnaris

flexor digitorium superficialis

Left: The exact same aerodynamic forces that determine whether an airplane will or will not fly act upon birds. Lift is provided by the inner part of the wing, which the bird constantly adjusts to maintain a regular force. The outer part of the wing, which moves similarly to a human hand, provides the thrust by the position of the primary feathers. Flight is achieved with lift plus thrust to overcome the natural drag of air and gravity on the body of the bird.

Riding the air

Many birds can take advantage of the special form of flight known as soaring, but hawks, eagles and vultures coasting in slowly rising circles while barely moving their wings are probably the most well-known for this ability. These birds are riding the updrafts created by thermals of warm air rising from the Earth's surface. It's common to see them doing this as they scan the ground for prey, but they also use this same principle in moving great distances along mountain ridges during migration.

What other purposes do feathers serve?

Flight is just one of the important functions served by feathers. They also are essential in protecting the bird from the elements, both temperature and precipitation, and from injury. Further, the feathers provide whatever camouflage the bird may have and contribute to much of its behavior.

Feathers are generally separated into five major types, based upon their functions:

● Contour feathers include most of the outer feathers that are visible on adult birds. They provide the general outline of the bird's body and "armor" against external forces. The wing and tail feathers involved in flight are specialized forms of contour feathers.

● Bristles are specially developed contour feathers that occur in limited locations on bodies of some species. Some of these locations are the eyelids, the toes and about the mouth, where the bristles appear to serve a sensory function.

● Down feathers are the soft white feathers that man has come to exploit in insulated vests and comforters. They naturally serve the same function on the bird's body.

● Semiplumes fall somewhere between contour feathers and down. They generally grow along the edges of the contour feathers and are mostly hidden beneath the contours. They allow for flexibility of the various parts of the bird's body, and provide additional insulation and, in waterbirds, additional buoyancy.

● Filoplumes are soft, hairlike feathers that generally grow in small groups at the base of contour feathers. They function with specialized corpuscles to sense movement or vibration of the contour feathers and pressure against the contours.

● Powder feathers look like some powdery material spread over areas of a bird's skin. Their exact functions have yet to be understood fully, although it appears they are involved in preening and, to some extent, in waterproofing.

How many feathers?

The number of feathers on an individual bird varies widely according to factors such as species, age, size and sex of the bird; season and geography. Those who have taken the time to count have found 1,500 to 3,000 feathers on most songbirds. A ruby-throated hummingbird holds the record for the smallest number on a bird that someone counted: 940. A whistling swan stands at the other extreme, again among only those species that someone has counted: 25,216.

Right: Although they're often difficult to differentiate, particularly on small birds such as the purple finch (far right), there are actually several different types of feathers on every bird, each type serving its own specialized function.

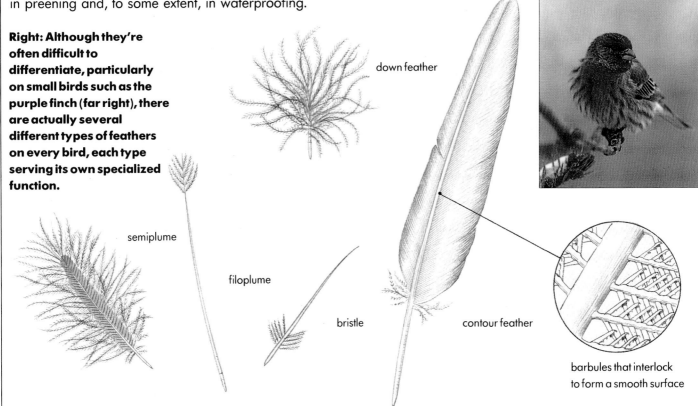

down feather

semiplume

filoplume

bristle

contour feather

barbules that interlock to form a smooth surface

Feather colors

The outward coloration of a bird, whether conspicuously bright or secretively camouflaged, is produced either by pigments in the feathers or by structural features of the feathers, or by combinations of the two.

● Pigment: Lipochromes produce blues, greens, yellow, oranges and reds, and are related to dietary elements. Melanins produce blacks, browns, red-browns and yellow, and may or may not be related to elements in the bird's diet. The complete absence of pigment results in albinism.

● Structural: Iridescent and non-iridescent colors are caused by reflective surfaces that interfere with light rays. Generally iridescent colors can be seen only from certain angles, but non-iridescent colors can be seen from any angle.

cedar waxwing

Anna's hummingbird

northern cardinal

15

How many bird species are there?

Of the 8,600-plus bird species that inhabit the Earth, about 650 breed in North America. Another 50 are "regulars," although they don't breed here. And, about 150 others have been recorded, although they are not residents of this continent.

It's been estimated that 100-200 species of birds remain to be discovered in this world. Probably none of them will be found in North America. The last new species for our continent recognized by the American Ornithologists' Union was the Colima warbler in 1889. Other birds since then generally have been determined to be subspecies of species already recorded.

How are the species defined?

Species differentiation is crucial in ornithology, and all of the other branches of biology, because it is the most basic category into which living things can be classified. The essential criterion for a species is that members breed exclusively with one another or so insignificantly with another species that traits are not lost.

Barriers to interbreeding

The barriers to interbreeding between species are substantial. Each species has its own courtship signals that pass between male and female and to which only members of that species are susceptible. This is generally known as species recognition. In addition, different species are ready for mating at different times and usually occupy different niches of the environment. And, of course, there are many genetic barriers in the path of the sperm from one species fertilizing the egg of another.

Below: The blue jay is a member of the crow family, Corvidae, which also includes ravens and magpies. Although the birds may differ greatly in outward appearance, they share many characteristics. As a group they appear to have evolved a very high degree of intelligence.

Left: The mourning dove is one of the most common backyard birds among the 650 or so species that breed in North America. The most common bird to ever inhabit the continent, the passenger pigeon, was a close relative of the dove until it was exterminated by humans.

Size records

Although many factors differentiate one species from another, among the most instantly obvious is size. The birds of North America range from the trumpeter swan, which can be more than six feet (1.8m.) long with a wingspan of as much as eight feet (2.5m.)and can weigh as much as 38 pounds (17kg.), to the calliope hummingbird, which extends only 2½ inches (6cm.) and weighs just ¹⁄₁₀ of an ounce (2.8g.). North America's largest bird is a far cry from the largest living bird on Earth, the African ostrich which can stand nine feet (2.7m.) tall and weigh more than 345 pounds (156kg.). At the other extreme, the North American record holder is quite close to the world's smallest bird, the bee hummingbird of Cuba, which measures no more than 2¼ inches (57mm.) and weighs about the same as the calliope.

Above: The American robin is the introduction to wild birdlife for many people at a very early age. The poor little, abandoned, fuzzy nestling that was laying pathetically under the tree is a common childhood memory for many of us.

Left: There are 25 species of the hawk family in North America, including the relatively common red-tailed hawk. Members of the family share the charac-teristic hooked bill, taloned toes and incredibly sharp eyesight that mark them as effective predators.

How many species have we lost?

We'll never be certain just how many species of birds vanished from the North American continent since the dawning of time. But we do know that within the past 200 years, we have lost five species: great auk, Labrador duck, heath hen, passenger pigeon and Carolina parakeet. North America has the worst record in this aspect of any continent on Earth.

How the species were lost

The last member of the flightless great auk clan died in Iceland in 1844, three years after the last record of any living specimen in North America. Commercial hunting for birds for market, oil and feathers (used in mattress stuffing) completely wiped out the species.

Sport and commercial hunting, as well as egg gathering, also played a large part in the demise of the Labrador duck by 1875. But scientific and historical proof has never been concrete enough to lay the total blame there.

The heath hen was actually an eastern race of the greater prairie chicken that still roams the west. Although a great deal was done to try to save the species toward its end, commercial hunting, conversion of its habitat to human settlements and the predations of domestic dogs, cats and vermin pretty much sealed the bird's fate by 1831. A small population survived on Martha's Vineyard, Massachusetts, for another hundred years — reaching a high of 2,000 — but the last heath hen was spotted in 1932.

The last passenger pigeon ended her solitary existence of 29 years on September 1, 1914, in a cage in the Cincinnati Zoo. She was the last of a species once so abundant that migrating flocks were estimated to number two billion and nesting colonies covered miles of trees with some individual trees holding more than 100 nests. Incredible numbers of the birds were shot for market at the same time that the species' woodland habitat was being converted en masse to open farmland.

The Cincinnati Zoo was also the last home of the Carolina parakeet, the last specimen of which also died in 1914. Although disease may have played a part in its final demise, sport hunting and destruction by farmers to protect their crops were the main culprits.

Endangered species

As of its last printing in 1990, the official U.S. Fish & Wildlife Services list of *Endangered and Threatened Wildlife and Plants* included 31 species of North American birds. That number represented only those species that had already gone through the multi-year process of study and consideration that leads to inclusion on the list. The waiting list for such study and consideration remains considerable.

Humanity has found many means to impact upon natural bird populations. The most common bird to ever inhabit Earth, the passenger pigeon (left), was lost to market hunting and habitat destruction. Introduced species, such as the house sparrow (right) had started the eastern bluebird on the same path until caring humans intervened.

Right: The Carolina parakeet was wiped out by the early 1900s by sport hunting and by farmers wanting to protect their crops. This is how Audubon saw the birds in 1825.

Carolina Parrot. Males 1, 2 & Young 3
PSITACUS CAROLINENSIS.
Plant Vulgo: Cuckle Burr

What is migration?

Although the experts may use the term migration for several different types of bird and animal movement, here we're referring only to that seasonal movement that involves about 80 percent of all bird species that breed in North America. Of those species, only about a quarter winter completely off the continent.

On the surface the reasons behind migration are obvious: the birds are escaping the harsh months of winter. But that answer doesn't even begin to explain why the birds don't simply stay to the south year-round and save the incredible amounts of energy required to migrate.

Why do birds migrate?

Science has yet to provide and prove a definitive answer, but two theories seem to be the most widely supported. The first holds that those species that migrate originated to the south thousands of years ago and moved northward to escape competition from other species. The lack of food for a brief period each year forces their return south. The second maintains nearly the exact opposite: during the last ice age half-a-million years ago, birds of North America retreated to the south as glaciers impacted their food supply, but retained an instinct to return as the ice left the land. Neither theory can account fully for certain aspects of migration.

A year-round event

We generally think of spring and fall as the migrating times because the most noticeable numbers of birds do pass through in those seasons. But, for various reasons, nearly the entire year sees some migrating species or populations. Within some species even the different sexes and ages migrate at different times.

Migration records

None of our backyard birds are extremists when it comes to migration. Most make the trip at 20-40 miles per hour (32-64 km. per hour), far below speeds of 100 miles per hour (160km. an hour) that have been recorded for some high-flying shorebirds. Most fly at altitudes of less than 100 feet (30m.) above the ground, while some of the species that migrate at night range from 3,000 to 5,000 feet (914-1,524m.). However, even that pales next to the record-holder — flocks of bar-headed geese reach 28,000 feet (8,534m.) when migrating across the Himalayas. And, although some swallow populations nest in northern Canada and winter in southern South America, the migrating distance for most of our backyard species is very short when compared to the 11,000 miles (17,699km.) that the arctic tern covers each fall and again in the spring.

Left: The sometimes huge Vs of Canada geese moving across the sky in late fall and early spring are the very embodiment of migration for many people. However, some local populations of the bird have given up their migratory ways for life in city parks and farmers' fields.

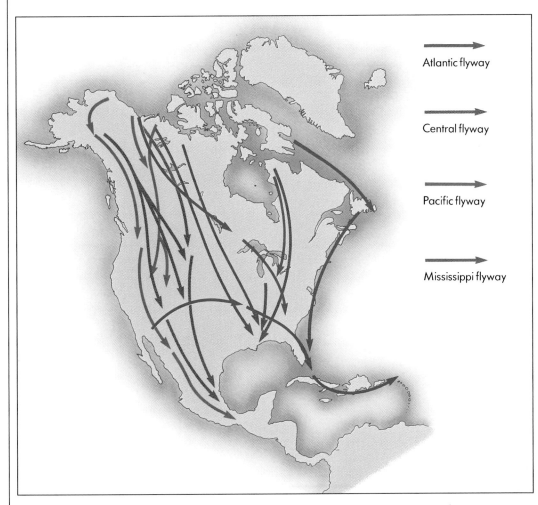

Atlantic flyway

Central flyway

Pacific flyway

Mississippi flyway

Left: Migratory bird species in North America generally follow one of four routes during their annual spring and fall flights. The route used is largely dependent upon the starting location of the bird, so it's common to find members of a single widespread species along all four routes.

Below left: Huge flocks of "blackbirds," including species such as grackles, red-winged blackbirds and European starlings, begin to gather in the north toward the middle of each fall in preparation for their annual move to the warmer climes of the South. Eastern bluebirds (below right), also migrate but in smaller groups.

How do I attract birds to my backyard?

Birds come to any backyard for three reasons: food, water and shelter. Generally the more of these three elements — in both quantity and variety — that a backyard provides, the greater will be its attraction for more birds and more species of birds.

Food and shelter

Start with the plants already growing there. View them in three distinct categories: flowers, grasses and similar herbaceous growth; shrubs and vines; and trees. Also consider their food-producing value and the thickness of the shelter they provide. A good manual about the plants under consideration can be helpful here; it's beyond the scope of this book to detail the varying benefits of the thousands of plant varieties you might encounter.

Next consider where you might like to add some new plants. Again, food-production and shelter are the prime considerations for attracting birds, but you'll find yourself much happier with the final results if you now also concern yourself with aesthetic appeal of the plants to humans.

Thirdly, give some thought to supplementing this natural array of food and shelter with artificial sources, including feeders and nest/roosting boxes. Across most of North America, such supplementary items will be necessary to maintain a regular population of visitors through the winter, when plants aren't producing their fruits, seeds or berries, and lose some of their shelter value.

Water

Never forget water. This is the one area that so many would-be backyard birdwatchers overlook. It also happens to be the one thing that can multiply the results of your efforts many times over. A wide array of bird baths, fountains and mini-ponds are both inexpensive and easy to install and maintain.

As you make your plans use graph paper to sketch everything out for yourself, maintaining an accurate scale that will both allow you to show the entire plan on one piece of paper but in enough detail to make it useful. A scale of one block on the graph paper to one square foot of property works well for most average backyards.

Backyard kits

There are two pre-packaged kits available to guide you through the planning and development of your own backyard wildlife habitat. Both offer several booklets about the various aspects of a backyard habitat, grid paper for your planning and landscape templates to help with your sketching. The two organizations that supply these are:

National Wildlife Federation, 1400 16th St., N.W., Washington, DC 20036.

Backyard Wildlife Association, 4920 Liberty Lane, Allentown, PA 18106.

Left: Water is a prime attraction for nearly all backyard bird species. It's also the element that is most often overlooked by newcomers to backyard wildlife gardening. Right: Varied nesting cover, ranging from tall weeds to shrubs and trees, will also bring many birds into the backyard, such as this female cardinal on her clutch of eggs.

What are the chief dangers to birds in my backyard?

No matter how much we might do to convert our backyards into natural habitats, the fact will always remain that these environments have been altered by humans. As such, the chief dangers to the birds that visit there are also related to us.

● More birds have died in the claws and jaws of domestic cats than from any other single cause in the backyard. As docile and tame as "Kitty" might seem, there is a cunning and able predator housed in that body and brain. Although some domestic cats have lost some of the skills of the hunt and are therefore unable to make the kill, all felines will go through some of the maneuvers.

Cats can be easily thwarted in most of their efforts to snatch up our songbirds. The local bird population soon learns to scatter at the first sound of a warning bell tied around the cat's neck. And through the careful placement of feeders and water sources, we can remove the potential for ambush and stalking.

● Our windows also have proved deadly to incredible numbers of backyard birds, particularly large windows that appear to offer a clear flight path. This, too, is an easily remedied situation. Hawk silhouettes are available from most garden supply companies for placement on the glass.

nest box protected by wire cage

hawk silhouette on glass window

Above: Feeders and boxes come in many sizes and designs to meet various needs, such as a hanging tube feeder for small birds and the purple martin colony (left).

What is a bird garden?

If you're open to something new and a bit different, birds will be happy to give you a hand in planting all of their favorite food plants in the backyard. All you'll have to do is pick the spot, get it ready and sit back to see what develops.

Wherever you want the birds to plant their garden, prepare a five-foot-wide (1.5m.-wide) strip of soil as if you were going to grow vegetables or flowers in late summer. The strip can be any length that you want, but remember the final result is going to be a tangled hedgerow-type affair of wild plants. This might mean it would be better suited for the very back of your yard, away from any neighbors who might not agree with your husbandry for wildlife.

Preparing the garden

Turn the soil, adding some humus and fertilizer (if your soil would normally need those enhancements to produce a satisfactory vegetable crop). Set a staggered line of fenceposts through the plot, at 10- to 20-foot (3-6m.) intervals and stretch heavy cord or wire between the posts, one strand at about five feet (1.5m.) off the ground and another at about one foot. Then just wait for the birds to do their part.

The strands of wire will attract birds to perch there and the birds, in turn, will "plant" the seeds of whatever plants they've been eating through their droppings. The variety of plants that will soon appear on the spot will include grasses, weeds, wildflowers, vegetables, domestic flowers, shrubs, vines and even small trees.

Allow all plants that come up in the first and second years to remain on the site for their full life cycle, including the all-important seeding period in late summer and fall. In the third year you can begin trimming and shaping your new hedgerow just as you would if you had purchased the shrubbery from a nursery. Wild plants such as these generally will respond with increased vigor after such a cutting.

Above: Seed-bearing plants like the moonseed are very attractive natural elements that can be added to most backyards to attract birds. Given the opportunity (as shown in the diagram below and explained at the left), birds will carry seeds they've eaten and "plant" them into their own natural garden.

Native plants

Native plants also will respond to the laissez-faire attitude toward backyard wildlife gardening. Plan for five five-foot-wide (1.5m.-wide) strips of soil next to one another. Till one strip each year in sequence, allowing the other four to do whatever they will. After the full five-year cycle you'll have a wild food patch with a smorgasbord of seed-bearing, bird-attracting, native plants, ranging from panic grasses, lamb's quarter and ragweed on the current strip to aster, goldenrod, milkweed and thistle on the third-year strip to small shrubs and tree seedlings on the fifth-year strip. Continue the tilling in sequence every year.

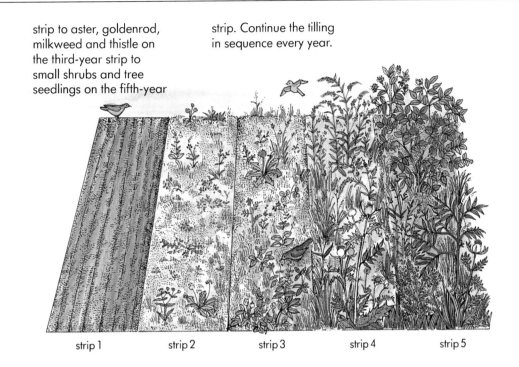

strip 1   strip 2   strip 3   strip 4   strip 5

Left: The growing interest in wildflower gardening across the country is proving to be very beneficial to a wide variety of bird species, which find ample natural food in the seeds that the wildflowers produce from late summer through fall.

Above: A very wide variety of flowers, including the trumpet creeper will attract hummingbirds, such as this ruby-throated male. Flowers in shades of red and tubular shapes have been found to be most attractive to all American species.

What are niches?

Through the winter woods, from the base of one tree to the base of the next, flits a flock of small birds: several chickadees, a few nuthatches, a creeper or two, a kinglet or two and a small woodpecker. At each stop the birds go through a seemingly disorganized session of activity before moving on. On close inspection we would find that each of the different species in that mixed flock was going about finding food in its own way, somewhat different from the food and methods of the others. This is the concept of "niche" in action.

A species' niche is its place within its ecosystem, how it relates to all other aspects of that ecosystem. The different species in our small mixed flock each fill their own niches differently to the niches of the others, sometimes in very minor ways, sometimes significantly. Because of this they generally don't compete with one another for any of the exact same requirements and can thus live together. This is known as ecological compatibility.

In addition to types of food and methods of feeding, a niche includes the species' requirements for shelter, water, nesting site, mates and any other intricate details of life. In general, species that compete directly for exactly the same niches are not found together in the same geographic locations.

Below: Crossbills are able to exploit pine cones as a food source because of their unique bill design. Many bird species cannot pry the tiny seeds from the tightly woven cones.

Left: Although the white-breasted nuthatch is often seen feeding with other species, it has found a different niche to exploit: moving upside down along the tree to probe from a different angle.

Eastern bluebird case study

Birds are very dependent upon their niches. The eastern bluebird is the premiere example of this. From the 1940s through the 1970s, the population of the birds plummeted at an alarming rate. Changing agricultural practices were eliminating the snags and old wooden fence posts that the birds needed for nesting, while introduced species were beating the bluebirds out for the nesting cavities that remained. The decline has been reversed in the past 10-15 years by backyard birders who erected thousands of bluebird nesting boxes throughout the species' former range, thereby replacing a crucial niche element that had been lost.

Right: The eastern meadowlark inhabits weedy locales, such as meadows, pastures and prairies, where it finds its diet of insects such as beetles and grasshoppers.

What are the best plants for birds?

Nearly any plant that provides food, directly in the form of seeds, berries or fruit or indirectly by attracting insects, or shelter will be of some use to bird species. Generally plants that provide both elements together will be of more use to more species. And a variety of plants that provide a variety of food and shelter types at various levels from ground to treetops will provide for and attract the largest number of birds.

The most effective varieties

It would be difficult to find any plant that hasn't been used by some bird species at one time or another, but there are those that do the job much more effectively for a wider spectrum of bird species. Some of the very best include:

● Deciduous trees — alder, ash, aspen, beech, birch, blackgum, black cherry, choke cherry, crabapple, dogwood, hackberry, hickory, maple, mountain ash, mulberry, oak, pecan, persimmon, Russian olive.

● Evergreen trees — Douglas fir, hemlock, holly, ironwood, juniper, larch, madrone, pine, red cedar, spruce.

● Deciduous shrubs — barberry, bayberry, beloperone, blackberry, blueberry, buffaloberry, butterfly bush, currant, dogwood, elderberry, firethorn, hawthorn, holly, honeysuckle, osoberry, privet, serviceberry, sumac, trumpet creeper, vibernum, Virginia creeper.

● Evergreen shrubs — buckthorn, cotoneaster, holly, huckleberry, inkberry, juniper, rhododendron, salal, yew.

● Ground covers and vines — bearberry, catbrier, cloudberry, dewberry, crowberry, grape, greenbrier, ground juniper, honeysuckle, pokeberry, rose, sarsaparilla, serviceberry, strawberry, Virginia creeper, wintergreen, yaupon.

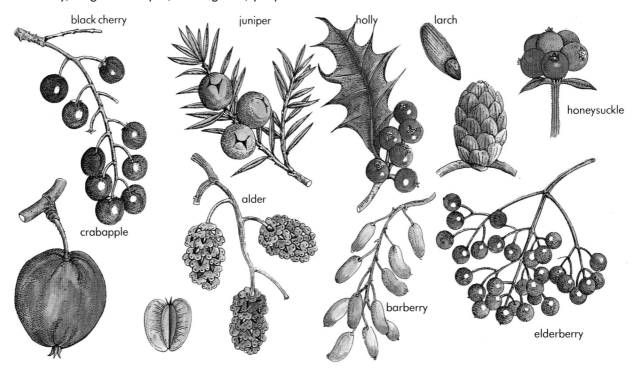

black cherry
juniper
holly
larch
honeysuckle
crabapple
alder
barberry
elderberry

Desirable weeds

Some of our most hated weeds also happen to be favored food plants among various bird species:
- Thistle — goldfinches love the seeds.
- Dandelion — seeds for finches and siskins.
- Chickweed — many songbirds love the seeds.
- Lamb's quarter — seeds for finches.
- Knotweed — seeds for many bird species.

thistle

dandelion

chickweed

lamb's quarter

knotweed

Above: A wide variety of plantlife holds special attractions for birdlife. For example, many plants that we consider weeds, such as thistle, are highly attractive to species like the American goldfinch. Right: the dead trees that most people quickly remove from their properties are also very attractive to a wide variety of species, such as the downy woodpecker.

Right: Fruit trees, like this crabapple, can act like a magnet for some species of birds that are difficult to attract through other measures, notably species such as the cedar waxwing.

What are the best bird foods?

This question can be answered with just the opposite information. The worst bird foods are those prepackaged collections of seeds and grains available at most supermarkets and department stores. They contain extraordinary amounts of grains and seed types that most birds do not want and will simply push out of the way to get to the few seeds they do want. And, when these mixes do contain any of the desired seed types, these are often of inferior grade.

Although some supermarkets and suppliers to supermarkets are making changes, the best seed mixes are available through nature stores, nurseries, garden centers, farm supply stores and home improvement centers. They often fill bins with a selection of the most preferred seed types and allow you to choose only those types that best suit the birds you want to attract. The pre-packaged mixes they offer generally contain much higher concentrations of seeds that the birds will actually use, but always be sure to read the label.

Seed mixes

The seed types you're looking for are oil-type sunflower seeds, black-stripe sunflower seeds and thistle or niger seeds. And, in smaller amounts, peanut kernels, red proso millet and white proso millet. An offering of all these types generally will attract any bird in the neighborhood that's inclined to come to feeders.

Avoid hulled oats, milo, peanut hearts, rice and wheat. These have no attraction for almost any bird species.

Below: Some species, like the mourning dove, will gather for nearly any type of seeds that are offered under any conditions. However, many bird species have much more exacting tastes that aren't met by many commercially available seed mixes.

Warning!

An often overlooked backyard danger to the birds lurks in the feeders and seeds we put out for them. Unused seeds, the hulls of eaten seeds, and the cracks and crevices of our feeders — particularly during periods of wet weather — can be breeding grounds for the fungus and bacteria that cause several avian diseases. Once started, these diseases can spread quickly and fatally through local bird populations. The best defense is removal of all seed particulars from the feeder every few days and regular cleaning with a bottle brush, water and a mild detergent.

Black oil-type sunflower seeds are the most attractive seeds for the widest variety of bird species. The nuthatch (left), and the tufted titmouse (above right) are just two of the dozens of species attracted to these seeds. Oil-type sunflower seeds may seem expensive in comparison to commercially available "supermarket" mixes, until the incredible waste of unwanted seeds in those "cheaper" mixes is taken into account.

Suet delicacy

Suet, the hard fat located around beef kidneys and loins, holds a special attraction for many bird species, including a good number that aren't generally attracted to other foods offered at the feeder. Especially in the winter, it offers a source of quick, high energy.

The most practical methods of offering suet are in the small, plastic-coated wire cages made specifically for that purpose or in small holes drilled in a vertical log. Other methods, such as hanging in a nylon mesh bag, are less efficient because they tend to wear out much more quickly and allow larger birds to steal the entire block of suet in a few trips.

log with drilled holes

wire cage suet feeder

What kind of feeders do I need?

The array of different feeder designs seems to grow every year, in the catalogs, at the garden centers, everywhere. There are larger feeders to accommodate more birds with various food selections, specialized feeders to bring in a special species or two, squirrel-proof contraptions that often are just as aesthetics-proof. As we approach the feeder season each year it's hard to believe that anyone can come up with yet another new feeder idea, but darn it if someone or several someones don't do exactly that.

Types of feeder

But there are only five basic designs that you need to be concerned with, and that's only if you want to attract every available and amenable species into your backyard. They are:
● Bin feeder: the traditional box atop a pole with a bin to hold the seed until it gradually flows into the feeder tray at the perching area below. This type caters for a large number of species, but can be taken over — generally for brief periods — by bully species, such as blue jays and grosbeaks.
● Hanging thistle feeder: a long, thin tube with tiny holes and perches interspersed along its length. The tube feeder, as it also is commonly called, serves the finch species very well.
● Hanging dome feeder: a round seed-container serving up larger seeds such as sunflower through several feeder holes equipped with perches at its base. A good, common feeder to serve many different species.
● Feeding table or platform: simply a large flat surface on a pole, legs or a stump, or even on the ground, where large quantities of seed are spread to serve considerable flocks of birds such as doves, grackles, and grosbeaks.
● Suet feeder: a plastic-covered wire cage or a mesh bag hung from a tree limb, or a log with holes drilled into it, where suet or peanut butter is offered for "special" species, such as nuthatches and woodpeckers.

A popular pastime

Backyard bird feeding didn't have much of a following until the late 1950s. Since then, however, the activity has mushroomed at an almost unbelievable rate. The most recent data indicates that more than one-third of all families in North America put out some seed every year. And their overall purchases for the activity now top the half-billion-dollar mark.

Left: Red is a very attractive color for all species of hummingbirds, such as the ruby-throated male shown here. However, red dyes should not be placed in sugar-water solutions offered to them, as such dyes can carry harmful chemicals. A red-tinted feeder fulfills the requirement just fine.

Above, right: Thistle or niger seeds, offered in mesh bags or in hanging tube feeders, are very attractive to many special bird species, such as pine siskins, American goldfinches and purple finches.

A wide variety of feeders, each offering a different type of seed or mix of seed, will attract the greatest variety of bird species. Platform, (far left below), and bin-type (above) feeders stocked with sunflower seeds and cracked corn work well for larger, bullying birds such as grackles, doves and jays. Hanging tube (left), and ball (below), feeders are more adapted for the needs of the smaller species, such as finches.

Why is water so important?

Birds take a very wide range of food types. Most species can make their meals on a variety of edibles from many sources. But all species need water. Only a few find all they need without visiting a regular water source. For the others, water has an incredible drawing power.

The backyard that offers a steady source of water along with food and shelter will always attract larger numbers and more species of birdlife than the backyard that offers only food and shelter, if all other conditions are equal. This is not a new idea. It's been preached by enthusiasts and experts for many years. And yet water is the most often overlooked feature in the backyard habitat.

From pans to ponds

In their quest for water, which at some times of the year can be more difficult to find than food, birds are not at all picky. They'll make eager use of everything from a pan of water set out each day to a full pond capable of supporting a flock of waterfowl.

About the only requirement of most backyard species is that the water source be rather shallow. Two to three inches is the maximum for most species. It should have gently sloping edges and a bottom that offers non-slip footing. An overhanging branch, not large enough to support a cat, or a thorny hedge within a few feet of the water source will give the bathing and drinking birds a greater sense of ease and security.

Below: Water is a crucial element in attracting any swallow species. The swift-flying little acrobats are almost always found near bodies of water, which they can be seen skimming both for drinks and for insects that fly near the surface of the water.

Left: Only a very few bird species are able to fulfill all their water needs from the foods they eat. Most species need to find water sources every day and will welcome any source you provide.

Right: Many species, such as the common grackle, seem to take great pleasure in bathing. They will spend lengthy periods in any shallow source of water as long as they are not threatened in any way.

Below: Traditional bird baths have been falling somewhat out of favor in recent times as the natural movement takes hold in backyard gardening. However, the pedestal-type bath continues to serve the needs of birds quite well.

Moving water feature

As attractive as any source of water is to so many different bird species, moving water is always much more appealing. The sound of even a slow, steady drip is as effective as any bird call on the market today.

It's easy and inexpensive to add this feature to any water source in the backyard. A plastic milk jug, with a tiny hole or two drilled in the bottom, filled with water and suspended a few feet above the water source performs just fine. Your garden hose, with its nozzle suspended (like the milk jug) and its water flow set to allow only a drip every few seconds, is another ready option.

How many kinds of nest are there?

At the most basic level there are as many different kinds of nest as there are species of birds. Under close scrutiny there is some slight difference to be found between the nests of even the most closely related species. However, as a practical matter there are a dozen different nest forms used by birds. They are:

- No nest; eggs laid on the bare ground or in a slight, scraped depression.
- Scraped depression with good amount of lining.
- Cup of various materials woven or otherwise worked together on the ground.
- Domed cup on the ground.
- Mound on land or rising out of water.
- Floating nest held in place by attachment to water plants.
- Burrow in the ground; either dug by the parent birds or dug and abandoned by other creatures.
- Cavity in a tree, fencepost, utility pole or similar upright wooden object.
- Platform of sticks in trees or shrubs.
- Cup of various materials in tree, lined with separate interior material or unlined.
- Baglike or cuplike structure hanging from a tree limb.
- Mud cup or burrow-like structure, manufactured by the birds.

In addition all 12 of these nest types have been used with the following variations:
- Colony nesting with several of the nests of the same species built in close proximity to one another.
- Group nesting in which several pairs of one species deposit their eggs in one nest and share incubating responsibilities.
- Previously occupied nest, either used after original builder has used it and departed, or as a depository for eggs left for the other species to hatch and foster.

Small deciduous rose-breasted grosbeak, brown towhee, house sparrow (cavity), black-capped chickadee (cavity), Carolina chickadee (cavity), Carolina wren (cavity), house wren (cavity), brown creeper (side of trunk), tufted titmouse (cavity), bushtit, American robin, wood thrush, brown thrasher, gray catbird, northern oriole, orchard oriole, Scott's oriole, common grackle, boat-tailed grackle, red-winged blackbird, Brewer's blackbird, European starling (cavity), cedar waxwing, black and white warbler (base of tree), white-eyed vireo, red-eyed vireo, American redstart, blue jay, black-billed magpie, tree swallow (cavity), violet-green swallow, eastern kingbird, least flycatcher, loggerhead shrike, northern flicker (cavity), downy woodpecker (cavity), pileated woodpecker (cavity), red-headed woodpecker, black-chinned hummingbird, ruby-throated hummingbird, Anna's hummingbird, mourning dove, common ground dove, screech owl (cavity), American kestrel (cavity).

Shrubby area common redpoll, blue grosbeak, indigo bunting, song sparrow, field sparrow, painted bunting, rufous-sided towhee, bushtit, veery, ruby-crowned kinglet, northern mockingbird, brown thrasher, gray catbird, common grackle, boat-tailed grackle, red-winged blackbird, Brewer's blackbird, white eyed vireo, black-billed magpie, loggerhead shrike, black-chinned hummingbird, Anna's hummingbird, mourning dove, common ground dove.

Grassland dickcissel, song sparrow, field sparrow, white-throated sparrow, white-crowned sparrow, savannah sparrow, hermit thrush, eastern bluebird (in cavity), western bluebird (in cavity), veery, brown thrasher, red-winged blackbird, Brewer's blackbird, eastern meadowlark, common yellowthroat, ring-necked pheasant, northern bobwhite, mallard (near water), Canada goose (near water).

Burrow, open ground dark-eyed junco, winter wren (in roots), hermit thrush, California quail, rock dove, killdeer.

Small conifer cardinal, pine siskin, chipping sparrow, black-capped chickadee (cavity), Carolina chickadee (cavity), Carolina wren (cavity), house wren (cavity), brown creeper (side of trunk), tufted titmouse (cavity), American robin, golden-crowned kinglet, ruby-crowned kinglet, common grackle, European starling (cavity), yellow-rumped warbler, black and white warbler (at base), white-eyed vireo, red-eyed vireo, American redstart, blue jay, gray jay, Steller's jay, tree swallow (cavity), least flycatcher, loggerhead shrike, mourning dove, common ground dove.

Large deciduous American goldfinch, house sparrow (cavity), black-capped chickadee (cavity), white-breasted nuthatch (cavity), red-breasted nuthatch (cavity), tufted titmouse (cavity), wood thrush, blue-gray gnatcatcher, northern oriole, orchard oriole, Scott's oriole, common grackle, boat-tailed grackle, Brewer's blackbird, European starling (cavity), cedar waxwing, yellow-throated warbler, black and white warbler (at base), red-eyed vireo, blue jay, American crow, tree swallow (cavity), violet-green swallow, eastern kingbird, least flycatcher, loggerhead shrike, northern flicker (cavity), downy

woodpecker (cavity), pileated woodpecker (cavity), red-headed woodpecker, ruby-throated hummingbird, screech owl (cavity), American kestrel (cavity), red-tailed hawk.

Large conifer purple finch, evening grosbeak, red crossbill, black-capped chickadee, white-breasted nuthatch (cavity), red-breasted nuthatch (cavity), tufted titmouse (cavity), golden-crowned kinglet, ruby-crowned kinglet, common grackle, European starling (cavity), yellow-rumped warbler, yellow-throated warbler, black and white warbler (at base), red-eyed vireo, blue jay, American crow, tree swallow (cavity), least flycatcher, loggerhead shrike, red-tailed hawk.

Special brown-headed cowbird, cliff swallow, barn swallow, purple martin, chimney swift, eastern phoebe.

Warning!

In the back portion of this book we've provided descriptions of the nests, and illustrations and descriptions of the eggs of the 100 most common backyard species across North America. This is interesting and helpful information, but used irresponsibly it could harm nesting birds, their eggs and their young. Please, always view an active nest from a distance. A pair of binoculars will provide as fine a close-up view as necessary. Never remove any surrounding vegetation to afford yourself a better vantage point. In this way you won't scare off the parent birds and you'll be treated to the miracle of hatching and rearing. Never remove or touch the eggs, and never try to touch a nesting bird.

What kind of houses do I need?

Except for properties that offer special environmental features — such as the open areas near water favored by purple martins — two types of bird house, or nest box, are all that the average backyard will ever need.

The first is the traditional box with a hole in one side. This is similar to the bird houses that many a youngster has constructed as one of his or her very first wood-building projects. However, while plans for many such bird houses call for a square structure, the cavity-nesting birds that will make use of the nest box in fact prefer more of a rectangle, with the vertical being the longer dimension.

The second is a simple flat platform attached to the side of a house or tree in a sheltered location. This type of arrangement is attractive to birds like the American robin, eastern phoebe and barn swallow, which can't make use of an enclosed nest box.

Nest box dimensions

According to the U.S. Fish and Wildlife Service, the following are the recommended nest-box dimensions for some common species. Species of similar size to those listed and that make use of similar nesting situations can also be expected to use the boxes.

traditional
enclosed nest box

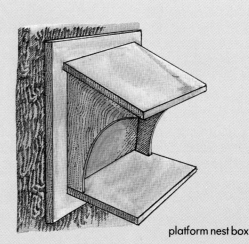

platform nest box

Species	Floor		Depth		Entrance above floor		Entrance diameter		Placement above ground	
	(in.)	(cm.)	(in.)	(cm.)	(in.)	(cm.)	(in.)	(cm.)	(in.)	(cm.)
American kestrel	11×11	28×28	12	30	9-12	23-30	3×4	7×10	20-30	51-76
American robin	6×8	15×20	8	20	no sides		no sides		6-15	15-38
Barn owl	10×18	25×45	15-18	38-46	4	10	6	15	12-18	30-46
Barn swallow	6×6	15×15	6	15	no sides		no sides		8-12	20-30
Black-capped chickadee	4×4	10×10	8-10	20×25	6-8	15-20	1⅛	2.9	6-15	15-38
Carolina wren	4×4	10×10	6-8	15-20	1-6	2.5-15	1½	3.8	6-10	15-25
Common flicker	7×7	18×18	16-18	40-46	14-16	36-40	2½	6	6-20	15-51
Downy woodpecker	4×4	10×10	9-12	23-30	6-8	15-20	1¼	3.2	6-20	15-51
Eastern bluebird	5×5	12×12	8	20	6	15	1½	3.8	5	12
European starling	6×6	15×15	16-18	40-46	14-16	36-40	2	5	10-25	25-63
Hairy woodpecker	6×6	15×15	12-15	30-38	9-12	23-30	1½	3.8	12-20	30-51
House wren	4×4	10×10	8-10	20-25	1-6	2.5-15	1-1¼	2.5-3.2	6-10	15-25
Screech owl	8×8	20×20	12-15	30-38	9-12	23-30	3	7	10-30	25-76
Tree swallow	5×5	12×12	6-8	15-20	5-6	12-15	1½	3.8	6-16	15-40
Tufted titmouse	4×4	10×10	8-10	20-25	6-8	15-20	1¼	3.2	6-15	15-38
White breasted nuthatch	4×4	10×10	8-10	20-25	6-8	15-20	1¼	3.2	12-20	30-51

Below: Some species, such as the eastern phoebe, prefer a nesting structure without enclosing sides.

Right: Many species will take advantage of nesting opportunities that their hosts never intended.

However, the majority of birds — including such varied species as the tufted titmouse (left) and the screech owl (right) — prefer enclosed nestboxes.

Position

Placement of the nest box is as important as design. For each of the species in the back section of this book that will use a nest box we've indicated preferred locations. However, beyond those individual guidelines, it is best to place no more than six nest boxes per acre (0.5 hectare) of ground. Research indicates that that is about the maximum density at which most cavity nesters will occupy any site. In addition, whenever multiple nest boxes are offered in a backyard they should be spread as far as possible from one another.

Why are eggs different colors?

Many wild birds do in fact lay pure white eggs, like those of domestic chickens. Among them the mourning dove, rock dove, screech owl, chimney swift, ruby-throated hummingbird, downy woodpecker and tree swallow.

Many more, however, lay very strikingly colored eggs, from the blue of the American robin's eggs to the creamy greenish brown of the eggs of the ring-necked pheasant to marblelike blotches and scrawls of brown, purple and black across a blue-green background on the eggs of the red-winged blackbird.

Camouflage

All the eggs of the ancestors of modern birds probably were white. Colors more than likely arose as the process of natural selection chose the mutations for the effectiveness of their camouflage. Although this probably can never be completely proven, egg-laying patterns among modern birds seem to support it. Although there are variations, white eggs tend to be laid by those species that nest in cavities or otherwise well-concealed nesting spots, or those that begin incubating their eggs as soon as the first is laid. In other words, the eggs of those species best served by camouflaging colors now have them.

This is not to say that there is not a great deal of variation in egg coloring within any given species, or even within a single clutch of one female. White eggs are regularly laid by birds that normally produce eggs of color.

Color and pattern

The color and color-pattern of an individual egg is determined by pigments known as porphyrins, which are produced in the female's body through the breakdown of hemoglobin from red blood cells that have ruptured. To get rid of these materials, the bird's body transforms them into bile pigments, which are moved to the uterus through the blood and deposited in the developing shell of the egg.

Size records

Egg size varies greatly among bird species, even in the sampling of 100 that we describe. The size of the bird laying the egg is the greatest factor determining the ultimate size of the egg. Of the birds included here — the most common backyard species — the smallest eggs are laid by the ruby-throated hummingbird, averaging 13×8.5mm, and the largest are laid by the Canada goose, averaging 3¼ × 2¼in. (85×58mm).

ruby-throated hummingbird egg

Canada goose egg

Below: The mud-grass nest and sky-blue eggs of the American robin have been many a child's introduction to this fascinating area of bird study over the years.

Below: Eggs are not entirely proportional to the body size of the female that lays them. These crow eggs, for example, are only about 5 percent of the female's body weight, while a house wren's eggs would be closer to 15 percent.

Above: Most bird species, such as these chickadees, have altricial nestlings, which are fully dependent upon their parents for all their needs.

Above: The larger egg in this red-eyed vireo nest is that of a brown-headed cowbird, which was left there by the female cowbird for the unwitting foster parent to raise.

Why do birds sing?

The tiny dickcissel leaps up onto a high perch and belts out his "dick-dick-sissel" over and over again, announcing his claim to this territory. If we stop to consider this for a moment, a smile is likely to emerge: such a miniscule ruler imagining himself in control of our backyard.

Courtship and mating

But to the birds, song is a very serious matter. For many species it is a critical factor during courtship and mating. Through his song — and in many species it is only the male that sings — the male announces his claim, both to rival males and potential mates. Neighboring males of many species thus establish their adjoining boundaries without ever resorting to physical confrontation. In some species, the male continues his singing through the nesting period as a communication link and bond builder with his mate.

Joy

In addition, there is a growing body of evidence that many species sometimes sing just because they feel like it. Suddenly, at some unpredictable moment, the male lets loose. The song, often accompanied by an ecstasy flight, seems to serve as a release of energy. Although I prefer not to attribute human traits to animals, there seems also to be an element of joy in these demonstrations.

Calls versus song

While not all bird species exhibit something that we would characterize as song, all species are capable of producing calls. These are usually of much shorter duration than song, usually a single note and rarely more than a half-dozen. Calls appear to be much more instinctual than song, with even the young birds responding in the expected manner. Many reasons have been documented for various calls of many different species, such as calling the flock together, warning of a predator's approach and begging parents for food. But for many species, the reasons behind much of their calling remain to be discovered.

Most passerine species, such as the dickcissel (above) and the indigo bunting (right), have distinct sounds to mark their territory and advertise their availability for mating. They generally employ these during the spring and summer. These primary songs, usually sung by the males, can be distinguished from the calls of both male and female throughout the year.

Above: The males of many species, such as this California quail, seek elevated and exposed positions from which to sing.

How do birds sing?

Mammals, including humans, produce their vocalizations in the larynx, which is located in the upper part of the trachea. Birds have this same adaptation, but the avian larynx produces no sounds. Instead, all bird songs and calls are produced in a separate organ, known as the syrinx. In most bird species, the syrinx is located where the trachea and bronchi meet.

Syringeal muscles
Pairs of muscles are attached to the syrinx, and it is these that control the bird's sound production. Songbirds have the greatest number of these muscles — nine pairs — while most non-songsters have only one or two pairs. The syringeal muscles, as these are known, work with elastic membranes in the syrinx and the bronchial air passages to produce and control sound: volume is raised or lowered with direction changes in the air passages; rhythm is produced by starts and stops in the flow of air; pitch is altered by relaxing or stretching the membranes in the syrinx; and tone is controlled through the rate of vibration of the membranes.

Because of this uniquely avian mechanism, bird sounds are little affected by mouth and nose. This is the reason why many species can produce their full repertoire without altering their beak position.

Inborn and learned
The ability to sing, thus, is inborn; part of the bird's physical make-up. The young of some songbird species have been recorded as singing a generalized song before they were even two weeks old. Singing the "correct" song(s) of the species, however, appears to be learned through hearing adult birds sing and then imitating them.

Song records
Although data on the number of songs sung during a given day of the singing period is far from complete for North American songbirds, some researchers have taken the time to make such counts for some species. One ornithologist counted 22,197 songs by a red-eyed vireo in one day in 1954. Another recorded that a song sparrow in Ohio sang 2,305 times in one day in May 1943. The same study counted 1,680 songs from one black-throated green warbler over a period of seven hours.

song sparrow

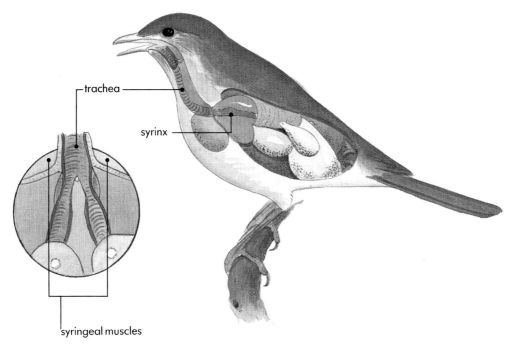

trachea

syrinx

syringeal muscles

Left: Birds do not have vocal chords. Instead, their song is produced by vibrating membranes in their voice boxes controlled by specialized muscles.

How can I identify bird sounds?

Today's generation of developing birders has an easier time learning the sounds of different bird species and the variations within a given species than any previous generation.

Written or verbal descriptions or imitations of bird songs and calls were the only means available to the general public until the past two-and-a-half to three decades. This is still one means of disseminating this information. This book includes a song description for each of the 100 species covered in the back section. However, I must admit, that sounds are the one area where there is a better way of providing information to learning birders.

Recorded bird-song

Recordings of the sounds of birds began to appear in the 1960s. One of the first widespread popular efforts was a 1964 set of six, six-inch-diameter, vinyl records included with the National Geographic Society's book *Song and Garden Birds of North America*. Since that time, technology has advanced a great deal. Now, each year seems to bring more sensitive, more discriminating electronic equipment to record and play back bird sounds.

As a result there are several editions of bird-song tapes, complete with accompanying guidebooks, commonly available through garden supply stores and nature center bookstores. Some cover more species; others offer special commentary or other variations. The most important criterion when selecting one for your own use is that the songs were recorded in the wild. This generally ensures that artificial influences had nothing to do with the sounds the birds produced.

Birding walks

Many local chapters of the national organizations listed later in this book, as well as non-affiliated local and regional organizations, sponsor regular birding walks. Some of these walks are designed specifically for teaching newcomers to the passion of birding. Such situations generally place you with experienced birders, who can instruct you about the species making the sounds you're hearing, and intricacies of the sounds that you might miss on your own, as well as general information about the birds.

Some species, such as the field sparrow (left), have very limited ranges of song. Others, like the mockingbird (below), are versatile enough to mimic dozens of songs.

Above: The ring-necked pheasant doesn't have a song, but the male is quite capable of proclaiming his dominance over territory with a resounding cackle.

Below: Northern bobwhites often roost in tight circles with rumps touching and eyes turned outward to watch for danger. They use specialized calls to gather.

The development of song in the chaffinch

Young songbirds are born with some song capacity and will naturally attempt singing on their own. However, they refine and develop their songs by listening to and mimicking adults of their species. The accompanying songograph of song by the same young bird at different points in its life, demonstrates this development from its beginning attempts in a subsong (top).

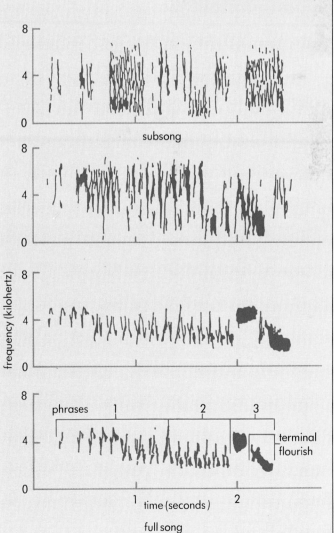

subsong

full song

Why does bird coloration vary so much?

Although shades and hues of browns, black and grays are the colors that occur most widely among North American birds, as a group they are the most colourful of all the continent's fauna. Every color of the rainbow can be found represented in at least a few bird species, and some of the brighter colors, such as yellows and reds, are widespread. (To understand the mechanisms involved in producing the different colors, refer to the section on bird feathers earlier in the book.)

Bright colors are most often found on animals that are active during the day, playing an integral part in their social signalling to others of their species. This is certainly the case with our bird species. To a certain extent, bright colors also play a part in the signals that many species give to other species, such as warning off would-be predators and confusing predators with a sudden flash of color.

The duller colors more often form camouflage protection from predators.

Social signalling

Whatever color a bird displays, it is the result of a conflict between the bird's social signalling needs and its methods of dealing with predators. The conflict is not something the bird itself has any influence upon. It is a generations-old process that has been decided, and continues to be decided, for the species as a whole through the process of natural selection.

In the brightly colored birds, this struggle has generally been decided on the side of communicating with its own species. This works for them because they tend to breed and nest in relatively safe locations, where camouflaging colors would not be as useful in thwarting predators. In addition, this provides part of the explanation for why the female counterparts of some brightly colored males are much duller, and why many brightly colored males lose their most glorious sheen outside the breeding season. Further, many of the more drably colored birds are among our most accomplished songsters, making use of that other means for communicating with rivals and potential mates.

Abnormal coloring

Some of the special conditions of bird coloration are:

- Albinism, which results in a white or whitish bird of a species normally colored differently, is caused by the lack of pigment. Partial albinism, in which splotches or patterns of white appear at some spots on the bird, is much more common.
- Melanism, which results in an abnormally black or dark bird, is caused by the presence of too much of the pigment melanin.
- Leucism produces an unusually pale bird, although not enough to be described as a true albino. It is caused by lower than normal amounts of all pigments.
- Schizochroism is caused by the lack of only certain pigments. It produces an abnormally colored or patterned bird.

Left: In many species there is a very distinct coloring difference between male and female. The northern cardinal demonstrates this very clearly. Such male-female color differences are generally most distinct during the spring mating season, when the male's coloring is part of his lure.

Clockwise from top left, painted bunting, young American robin, common grackle. For various reasons, ranging from protection through camouflage to mate attraction, every color of the rainbow can be found in the world of birds, even among the limited selection that we have come to refer to as our common backyard species.

How else can I identify birds?

The colors and patterns of a bird's overall plumage are the ultimate, visual determinants of an individual bird's exact species. However, many birds are not prone to sitting still long enough for all of their colors to be fully recognized.

To make quicker identification in the field possible, birders have come up with a system based on the field marks of birds. Although entire books have been written about this system, for the amateur birder it can be a much more simple matter.

Size and physique

First, note the relative size of the bird, in comparison to the size of a few birds you are familiar with — perhaps a house sparrow, a robin, a blue jay and a crow. Where on that scale does this new bird fall? Now, develop your description of the bird's physique. Is it slender or plump? Stooped or erect?

Bill and tail

Note the size and shape of the bird's bill. Is it most like a needle, a chisel, a spear, a hook, a rounded triangle, an upside-down scoop or a spoon?

Next, check the tail. Is it long or short? Is it forked or notched? Is it rounded, square or wedge-shaped? Ask the same questions about the wings.

Finally, note any special features of the bird. This might include wing or tail bars, eyerings or lines, crests or especially notable areas of color.

With all this information in mind — or better yet, written in a notebook — it will be a simple matter to locate the few birds that have all of these field marks in your field guide and then make a final determination based on your memory of the bird's color. Of course, if the bird remains in sight after you've noted the field marks, begin noting its overall coloration and even start paging through your field guide.

Field guides

Field guides offer a very wide range of options to potential buyers. The most notable difference, and one which affects how you use the guide in the field, lies in how the guide pictures the birds.

Some rely on photos to make identification. Others rely on artwork. The decision on which to use is ultimately one that the individual guide-user must make for him or herself.

There are arguments on both sides of the issue. Some claim that photographs provide a more accurate overall representation of the birds. Others point out that the artist's representations allow for more fully depicting and highlighting special identification points on each species.

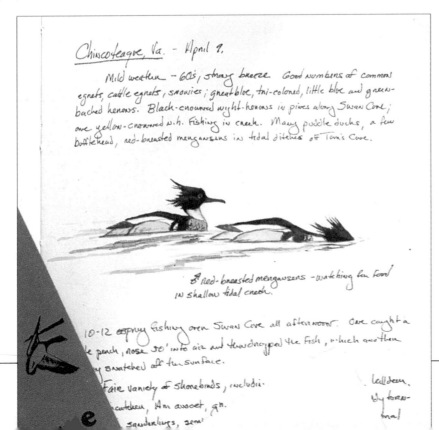

Left: All birdwatchers should keep some sort of journal or log in which to record observations and thoughts about the birds they observe. Important contributions have been made to the scientific understanding of birds through such observation. Besides, it's just plain fun.

Above and upper right: The house sparrow is one of the most common backyard birds throughout much of the continent. So much has been written about the species that it is an excellent selection on which to test your powers of observation and recording, with plenty of comparison material available.

Right: Although some people with backyard bird feeders tend to disapprove of the presence of predators such as the American kestrel in their neighborhoods, a more natural approach is to accept the bird as a part of the real world and observe its actions and interactions.

Above: The careful watcher will be treated to many unusual scenes that the less observant person may not even know ever happened. Egg-stealing and eating is such an activity, engaged in by many different species of birds, notably members of the crow family.

What do I need to get started in bird watching?

Bird watching, or birding as the pursuit has come to be called in more recent years, is one of the most inexpensive pursuits to get started. A field guide is the only truly essential piece of equipment. And for those who want to test the waters before spending anything, the local library generally offers several versions for loan at absolutely no cost.

Binoculars

However, even most beginners find they enjoy the pursuit much more from day one if they also have a pair of binoculars. These optical instruments offer much more detailed observation of the birds and their behavior. Many choices and price ranges are available, and manufacturers all tout a bewildering array of special features.

Below: When choosing binoculars the important criteria are shown here.

Power: the magnification rate of the binoculars. This is indicated by a set of numbers somewhere on the housing, such as 6×30 or 7×35. The first number is the power. Binoculars with a power of 7× magnify what they're focused on seven times. Most backyard birders prefer 7× or 8×.

Field of view: the width of the image you see through the binoculars, normally expressed on the housing as degrees. However, it actually represents the width in feet when viewed at 1,000 yards. To convert the degree number to this latter figure, multiply the degree number by 52.5. Wide fields of view offer easier location of birds.

Exit pupil: the bright area you see in the lens when you hold the binoculars at arm's length and look into the eyepieces. The larger the exit pupil, the brighter the image that the binoculars will provide. Exit pupils of 2-4mm are recommended for bright light situations, 4-5mm for shaded areas and more than 5mm for use in the low light of dawn or dusk.

Objective lens: represented by the number after the ×. This is the size of the lens. The larger the lens, and the number representing it, the better the light-gathering capacity of the binoculars.

Focus: center-focus allows for focusing on much closer objects than individual eyepiece-focus.

Mechanical movements: the parts of the binoculars should operate smoothly.

Lens coating: the coating that has (or has not) been applied to the optics of the binoculars to reduce light reflection and glare within the lens. The coating, which all quality lenses have, shows up as purple or amber when the binoculars are used under florescent light.

Above and right: Birdwatching has really come into its own in the past few decades. No longer is it the realm of stereotypical, pith-helmeted fanatics. Today, people from all walks of life engage in the activity, which has become a multi-million dollar business with organizations of thousands of members.

Birding organizations

Here is a partial list of North American organizations involved particularly with birds and birding:

National Audubon Society, 950 Third Ave., New York, NY 10022. Founded: 1905. Membership: 555,000.

Canadian Nature Federation, 450 Sussex Drive, Ottawa, Ontario, Canada K1N 6Z4. Founded: 1971 (from the Canadian Audubon Society). Membership: 36,000.

American Ornithologists' Union Inc., National Museum of Natural History, Smithsonian Institution, Washington, DC 20560. Membership: 5,000.

American Birding Association, P.O. Box 6599, Colorado Springs, CO 80934.

There are hundreds more organizations, which to a lesser or greater extent are interested in and involved with birds, birding and bird-related issues. The best guide to all of these organizations is the annual *Conservation Directory* published by the National Wildlife Federation, 1400 16th St., N.W., Washington, DC. 20036-2266.

Joining an organization

An organized approach to birding, to the sharing of information of interest to birders, to the support of research about the birds and their behaviors, to the protection of birds, has a rich and long-standing tradition.

The first bird-enthusiast organizations were formed to support and share research by the scientists of the day. The Deutsche Ornithologen-Gesellschaft was founded in 1853, followed in 1859 by the British Ornithologists' Union. Among the primary functions of these first bird organizations was the publication of journals to maintain and disseminate new findings about the birds, during this peak period of discovery.

Organizations of a more generalist bent saw their beginnings more than a century ago to press for an end to the use of bird feathers in the hat. These included the likes of the Massachusetts Audubon Society, founded in 1896, and the Society for the Protection of Birds (today the Royal Society for the Protection of Birds), organized in 1889 in the UK.

Although bird organizations have been founded ever since these first groups pulled together, the post-World War II period has proven to be the heyday for a mushrooming of numbers of new organizations. This phenomenon has taken place around the world, largely in connection with the growth of interest in birding by the general public.

How can I take professional-quality bird photos?

When considering bird photography, there are a few things you must understand about those wonderful, tack-sharp, insightful images you see in magazines and books such as this. First, these images are mostly made by professional photographers, using some pretty expensive and specialized equipment. And, equally important, these photographers are ready, willing and able to spend the time — often surprising amounts of time — needed to get these special shots.

Professional equipment

The 35-mm single lens reflex camera is the choice of these professionals. This type of camera allows the subject to be viewed directly through the viewfinder, is lightweight and compact, and above all allows for easy changes of lens.

It is the lens that really makes the image. For example, most point-and-shoot cameras widely used by non-professionals offer a lens somewhere in the range between 30 and 70mm. By comparison, normal eyesight is represented by a 50-mm lens. Many of the close-up shots that show the details of a bird or its behavior are taken with lenses in the 300-500-mm range. And, even with these powerful lenses, many of the professionals use blinds and other special arrangements to get even closer to their subjects.

Given all this, is it any longer a mystery why those photos you've been taking with your point-and-shoot camera, of birds that you can see perfectly well with your naked eyes, have been showing nothing more than a detail-less speck?

Getting closer

However, this does not mean that you can't get in on some fairly nice bird photography without investing thousands of dollars in professional-level camera equipment. Simply by

Below, left: Only with a camera equipped with a very strong telephoto lens, or under captive conditions, can anyone expect to take photos such as this of an American kestrel eating a freshly captured butterfly. The lens used for such a photo will generally cost several thousand dollars.

Setting up a blind

Completely acceptable — even publishable — photos can be produced through the use of blinds without a super-telephoto lens. Reasonably priced, medium telephotos will give very good results under such a set-up.

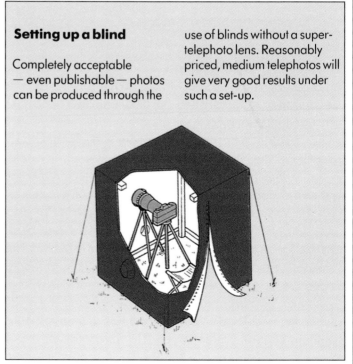

Left: A knowledge of what a particular bird likes to eat, where it prefers to roost and such other natural history facts are as useful to the professional wildlife photographer as expensive equipment. Cedar waxings, for example, will exhibit very predictable behavior once they have been located in a given area, allowing even the amateur ample photo opportunities.

getting closer to your subject — always closer than you think you need to — you will produce much better photos that show much more of the subjects you're trying to capture. By the way, this applies to photos you take of your family, friends and vacation spots as well.

Of course, getting close to birds generally requires a bit of special effort on your part. You might try propping up a drab-colored sheet in a small circle or square close to your bird feeders as a cheap-and-easy blind. Or, you might consider moving your feeders closer to a window and shooting your photos from inside the house. If you try this through the glass of the window, you will be happier with the results if you make certain that the plane of the camera is the same as the glass.

Zoom lenses

Another of the relatively less expensive options might be for you to purchase one of the newer point-and-shoot cameras that come equipped with zooming lenses that can reach up into the 210-mm range and above. Lenses of that power begin to stretch your capability and some of these cameras do produce very nice photos. However, when you begin considering these you want to compare their prices to those of some low-end 35-mm SLR systems with even more powerful lenses.

BIRD DIRECTORY

How to use the directory

THE FOLLOWING pages are designed to help you to quickly and accurately identify the most common backyard birds of North America. When you encounter a new bird species begin your identification process with the large artwork, then move to the more detailed elements provided under the Spotter's Checklist. The quick reference symbols and the succinct text will assist in a speedy verification of the species. When you have arrived at an identification turn to the longer text portion of the entry and gain additional insights into the life of the species you've just observed.

Special Note: We've provided detailed artwork and descriptions of the eggs and nests of each species. These should be observed only at a distance, using binoculars.

Egg
All eggs are shown in actual size and color. We've tried to show the typical egg for each species, but within any given species the coloring and pattern of the eggs can be highly variable from one female to the next.
Special Note: Observe eggs only from a distance with binoculars.

Feather
This is a typical contour feather, which gives the bird its general outline. It is shown actual size.

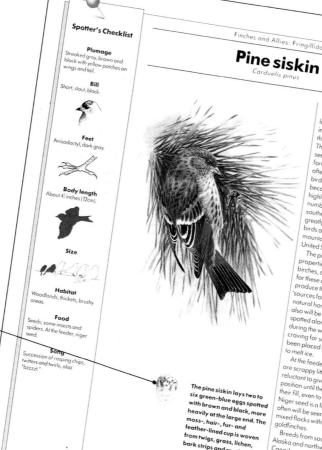

Spotter's Checklist

Plumage
Streaked gray, brown and black with yellow patches on wings and tail.

Bill
Short, stout, black.

Feet
Anisodactyl, dark gray.

Body length
About 4½ inches (12cm).

Size

Habitat
Woodlands, thickets, brushy areas.

Food
Seeds; some insects and spiders. At the feeder, niger seed.

Song
Succession of rasping chips, twitters and twirls; also "bzzzzt."

Finches and Allies: Fringillidae

Pine siskin
Carduelis pinus

THE PINE siskin is naturally a resident of more northerly latitudes, but is seen regularly in winter backyards throughout the United States. This usually occurs when the seed crops of its northern forest fail, which happens just often enough to qualify the bird for backyard status. But because crop failures are highly regional in nature, the number of birds making such southerly forays will vary greatly from year to year. The birds also are resident in the mountains of the western United States.

The pine siskin favors properties with alders, birches, cedars and hemlocks for these are the trees that produce the main food sources for the bird in its natural home. The pine siskin also will be commonly spotted along roadways during the winter, satisfying its craving for salt, which has been placed on the pavement to melt ice.

At the feeder, pine siskins are scrappy little birds, reluctant to give up their position until they've eaten their fill, even to larger birds. Niger seed is a favorite. They often will be seen traveling in mixed flocks with American goldfinches.

Breeds from southern Alaska and northwestern Canada south throughout the western U.S. and east through southern Canada and northern U.S. Winters throughout the U.S. and along the Canadian Pacific Coast.

The pine siskin lays two to six green-blue eggs spotted with brown and black, more heavily at the large end. The moss-, hair-, fur- and feather-lined cup is woven from twigs, grass, lichen, bark strips and rootlets. The nest is usually on the branch of a conifer 6 to 35 feet (1.8-10.5m) off the ground.

Finch

Com

THE COMMON redpoll is another of the northern finches that backyard birders in the United States are most likely to see when the seed crops of the northern forests fail. Also, like the pine siskin and others of this ilk, the number of common redpolls in these shifts to the south will vary from few to thousands.

Backyards with patches of weeds left standing throughout the winter are particularly attractive to these small birds. In such a situation, a flock of common redpolls will attack the weeds in a constant wave of motion, as the dried seed pods and flowers are shredded. The birds then drop to the ground to feed on the seeds that have showered there. Common redpolls spend a great deal of time on the ground, usually in thick patches of weeds.

Although they are hardy little birds, well able to sit out the worst winter storms, brush piles of evergreen branches or discarded Christmas trees are favored roosting areas for the night.

Probably because of its limited exposure to humans, the common redpoll is an open, trusting bird in the backyard. It allows much closer approach that most other finches and can occasionally be conditioned to take seed — particularly niger seed — from the hand.

Breeds throughout Alaska and northern Canada. Winters from Alaska and central Canada south to the Carolinas and California.

Bills

Short, rounded. Example: Dark-eyed junco. Seed- and fruit-eater.

Long, sharp. Example: Carolina wren. Insect-eater.

Long, needlelike. Example: Ruby-throated hummingbird. Nectar-eater.

Large, broad and stout. Example: American crow. Catholic diet.

Long, flat, rounded. Example: Mallard. Waterfowl.

Heavily hooked. Example: American kestrel. Bird of prey.

Short, stout. Example: Northern cardinal. Seed-eater.

Short, sharp. Example: Common redpoll. Seed-eater or insect-eater.

Large, conical. Example: Evening grosbeak. Seed-eater.

Crossed mandibles. Example: Red crossbill. Very specialized seed-eater.

Small, conical. Example: Brown towhee. Seed- and fruit-eater.

Long, sharp. Example: Northern mockingbird. Insect-eater.

Feet

Anisodactyl. Example: American robin. The most common foot arrangement; perching birds.

Zygodactyl. Example: Downy woodpecker. Climbing, clinging birds.

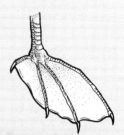

Palmate. Example: Mallard. Water birds, adapted for swimming and diving.

Pamprodactyl. Example: Chimney swift. Very specialized arrangement; clinging to sheer sides.

gillidae

dpoll

Spotter's Checklist

Plumage
Streaked brown and buff with red cap, darker chin and rose breast. Female similar but lacks rose breast.

Bill
Short, sharp, silvery.

Feet
Anisodactyl, dark gray.

Body length
About 5½ inches (13cm).

Size

Habitat
Brushy areas, weedy areas, thickets.

Food
Seeds and fruits and berries; insects and spiders when nesting. At the feeder, niger and oil-type sunflower seeds.

Song
Series of soft twittering and rattling.

mon redpoll lays
ix pale green to
-green eggs
th brown in a
ned cup of grass
ts on the ground
bush or small
est is usually no
20 feet (6m) off

Body length
Measured from tip of bill to tip of tail.

Size
For quick comparison to some of the most common birds on the continent: American goldfinch, house sparrow, starling, American robin, grackle, and American crow. If a bird is between two sizes, both are shaded.

Spotter's Checklist

Plumage
Bright red with black face. Female buff brown with red at crest, eyes, tips of wings and tail.

Bill
Short, stout, red.

Feet
Anisodactyl, gray.

Body length
About 7½ inches (19cm).

Size

Habitat
Brushy areas, thickets, woodland edges.

Food
Seeds, some insects and spiders. At the feeder, oil-type sunflower seed.

Song
"Wheat-wheat-wheat;" also "chip."

Northern cardinal
Cardinalis cardinalis

The northern cardinal lays two to five gray- to green-white eggs spotted and blotched with brown, gray and purple. The grass- and hair-lined nest, loosely woven of twigs, leaves, bark strips and weed stalks is usually placed in a thick coniferous tree or shrub from 5 to 10 feet (1.5-3m) off the ground.

THE BRIGHT red plumage of the northern cardinal, brightening the otherwise mostly dismal gray and white of the landscape, has made this species a favorite among winter bird feeders. To some extent, the cardinal realizes that its brilliant coloring makes it stand out as a target for predators and the bird has a shy and retiring personality. It will be a regular at the backyard feeder, often making several trips a day, but it is generally most at ease when there is thick cover nearby. Evergreen trees and shrubs, and hedgerows, are particularly attractive.

Both sexes are accomplished singers and their song can be heard nearly any time of the year. The male sings primarily in courtship and for territorial reasons, while the female's song is mostly in communication with her mate. The pair generally forms a long-term bond that extends across the years, rather than only during the mating season.

Resident throughout the eastern half of the U.S., western Texas, Arizona and southern California, the cardinal has been expanding its range northward for several decades, taking advantage of the favorable habitat provided by suburban development. Increased backyard feeding also has made it possible for more of the birds to endure more northerly winters.

American goldfinch
Carduelis tristis

THE BRILLIANT lemon-yellow coloring of the male goldfinch is reason enough for many backyard birders to maintain a hanging tube-feeder. Although flocks of the small finch will frequent such feeders year-round, it is only during the spring-through-early-fall period that the male gains his wonderful plumage. From mid-fall through winter, he'll appear nearly as dull as his olive-toned mate. The male American goldfinch goes through one of the most marked seasonal color changes of any of our backyard birds.

The species also is one of our latest to nest each year, generally putting off family duties until August. This coincides with a bountiful period of seed production by the various seed-bearing weeds that provide the primary food source for the bird, both adults and their offspring; regurgitated, partially digested seeds make up a major portion of the nestling's diet. The much-hated thistle is a particular favorite, and a single plant may be seen holding and feeding a half-dozen or more goldfinches at one time.

Breeds throughout the northern half of the U.S. and southern Canada. Winters throughout the U.S., except for much of the Great Plains and Rockies.

The American goldfinch lays four to six pale blue-white eggs in a down-lined (thistle or cattail) cup woven from strips of plant material. The nest is usually in the fork of a tree limb from 1 to 30 feet (0.3-9m) off the ground.

House finch
Carpodacus mexicanus

Spotter's Checklist

Plumage
Streaked gray-brown and buff with red head, breast and rump. Female similar but without red.

Bill
Short, stout, gray.

Feet
Anisodactyl, gray-brown.

Body length
About 5½ inches (14cm).

Size

Habitat
Residential areas.

Food
Seeds and fruits and berries; some insects and spiders when nesting. At feeder, sunflower and niger seed.

Song
"Zzree-zzree;" also high-pitched warble; also "cheep."

IT'S THE rare backyard feeder in the northeastern United States that does not see regular visits from a flock or two of house finches. In some parts of the region, the small red-tinted bird is among the most common backyard residents. However, this is a relatively recent phenomenon, and one that was brought about by humans. In the early 1940s, pet shops in New York City were discovered illegally selling house finches as pets. When authorities began cracking down on the practice, at least one pet shop owner freed his supply. From those few birds, the eastern population has grown. Without intervention, the house finch still would be a resident of only the western third of the country.

As an introduced species, the house finch in the east seems to rely heavily upon people for its food. It is nearly always found in close proximity to human habitation. Nesting materials, such as mesh bags of hair and bits of yarn, and nesting baskets, will readily encourage the birds to set up housekeeping in the backyard in the spring. The western population occurs across a much wider cross-section of native habitat than the introduced eastern population, but includes developed areas as well.

Resident throughout mid-Atlantic, northeastern and western half of the U.S. north into British Columbia.

The house finch lays two to six blue-green eggs lightly spotted with black in a gathering of twigs, grasses and debris in some form of cavity.

58

Purple finch
Carpodacus purpureus

ALTHOUGH THE purple finch is a relatively common species throughout its range, many reported sightings are actually of the even more common house finch. The two species are quite similar in appearance, although the purple finch generally displays more red, and both are ready feeder visitors. In general, the purple finch is duller and has more extensive red coloring than the house finch.

Large flocks of purple finches will frequent feeders regularly from late fall through early spring, virtually taking over the sites and dominating them for periods of several hours. The small birds will consume an impressive amount of seed, particularly oil-type sunflower seeds, on every visit. Smaller flocks will continue to visit the feeder throughout the rest of the year.

Even larger flocks are common sights in the southen United States during their fall migration, when the birds that have spent their summer across southern Canada move to winter in the warmer climes to the south. Those birds that spend their summers in the northeast and along the west coast, however, are generally permanent residents.

Breeds from central Canada south along the Pacific Coast in the west and south to New Jersey in the east. Winters throughout eastern half of the U.S. and western quarter.

The purple finch lays three to five green-blue eggs spotted and scrawled with brown and black in a grass- and hair-lined cup woven from twigs, bark strips, weed stems and grass. The nest is usually placed in the fork of a conifer 5 to 60 feet (1.5-18.2m) off the ground.

Spotter's Checklist

Plumage
Dull red with gray-brown tint on wings and tail. Female and young much browner with noticeable pale eyebrow.

Bill
Short, stout, gray.

Feet
Anisodactyl, gray-brown.

Body length
About 6 inches (15cm).

Size

Habitat
Woodlands, residential areas with trees.

Food
Seeds and fruits and berries; some insects and spiders. At the feeder, niger seeds.

Song
Warble, ending in a downward trill.

Pine siskin
Carduelis pinus

Spotter's Checklist

Plumage
Streaked gray, brown and black with yellow patches on wings and tail.

Bill
Short, stout, black.

Feet
Anisodactyl, dark gray.

Body length
About 4¾ inches (12cm).

Size

Habitat
Woodlands, thickets, brushy areas.

Food
Seeds; some insects and spiders. At the feeder, niger seed.

Song
Succession of rasping chips, twitters and twirls; also "bzzzzt."

The pine siskin lays two to six green-blue eggs spotted with brown and black, more heavily at the large end. The moss-, hair-, fur- and feather-lined cup is woven from twigs, grass, lichen, bark strips and rootlets. The nest is usually on the branch of a conifer 6 to 35 feet (1.8-10.6m) off the ground.

THE PINE siskin is naturally a resident of more northerly latitudes, but is seen regularly in winter backyards throughout the United States. This usually occurs when the seed crops of its northern forest fail, which happens just often enough to qualify the bird for backyard status. But because crop failures are highly regional in nature, the number of birds making such southerly forays will vary greatly from year to year. The birds also are resident in the mountains of the western United States.

The pine siskin favors properties with alders, birches, cedars and hemlocks for these are the trees that produce the main food sources for the bird in its natural home. The pine siskin also will be commonly spotted along roadways during the winter, satisfying its craving for salt, which has been placed on the pavement to melt ice.

At the feeder, pine siskins are scrappy little birds, reluctant to give up their position until they've eaten their fill, even to larger birds. Niger seed is a favorite. They often will be seen traveling in mixed flocks with American goldfinches.

Breeds from southern Alaska and northwestern Canada south throughout the western U.S. and east through southern Canada and northern U.S. Winters throughout the U.S. and along the Canadian Pacific Coast.

Common redpoll
Carduelis flammea

THE COMMON redpoll is another of the northern finches that backyard birders in the United States are most likely to see when the seed crops of the northern forests fail. Also, like the pine siskin and others of this ilk, the number of common redpolls in these shifts to the south will vary from few to thousands.

Backyards with patches of weeds left standing throughout the winter are particularly attractive to these small birds. In such a situation, a flock of common redpolls will attack the weeds in a constant wave of motion, as the dried seed pods and flowers are shredded. The birds then drop to the ground to feed on the seeds that have showered there. Common redpolls spend a great deal of time on the ground, usually in thick patches of weeds. Although they are hardy little birds, well able to sit out the worst winter storms, brush piles of evergreen branches or discarded Christmas trees are favored roosting areas for the night.

Probably because of its limited exposure to humans, the common redpoll is an open, trusting bird in the backyard. It allows much closer approach than most other finches and can occasionally be conditioned to take seed — particularly niger seed — from the hand.

Breeds throughout Alaska and northern Canada. Winters from Alaska and central Canada south to the Carolinas and California.

The common redpoll lays three to six pale green to deep blue-green eggs spotted with brown in a feather-lined cup of grass and rootlets on the ground or in a low bush or small tree. The nest is usually no more than 20 feet (6m) off the ground.

Evening grosbeak
Coccothraustes vespertinus

Spotter's Checklist

Plumage
Brown-tinted head fading into yellow on shoulders and breast, yellow eyebrow, black wings and tail with white patches. Female similar but gray tinted.

Bill
Large, cone-shaped, greenish yellow.

Feet
Anisodactyl, pink.

Body length
About 8 inches (20cm).

Size

Habitat
Coniferous woodlands; residential areas and deciduous woodlands in winter.

Food
Seeds and fruits and berries. At the feeder, sunflower seeds.

Song
Succession of brief and abrupt whistles.

The evening grosbeak lays two to five blue-green eggs blotched and spotted with brown, gray and purple in a rootlet-lined cup loosely woven from twigs, moss and lichen. The nest is usually in a conifer 20 to 60 feet (6-18.2m) off the ground.

THIS IS an expensive bird at the backyard feeder, arriving in large flocks, each member of which eats large quantities of sunflower seeds over relatively short periods of time and in the process pushes nearly as much from the feeder. They also are bullies and tend to spend long periods at the feeder, during which time many smaller birds have a hard time feeding among them. However, for many backyard birders, the coming of these big, bright birds is an eagerly awaited event of late fall or early winter. That arrival varies from no birds one year to huge flocks the next, depending upon the cone crop in their natural forest homes in Canada and the western U.S. However, this natural movement seems to have been increased greatly by the thousands of new bird feeders erected throughout the eastern half of the country in recent decades.

A special feeding method for these eager eaters is to plant sunflowers in the backyard and allow the plants to retain their dried, seed-laden heads into the winter. The seed heads also might be removed and offered at the feeding site. In either instance, the evening grosbeaks will not hesitate to pick their own meal.

Breeds from central Canada south into New England in the east and Mexico in the west. Winters in southern Canada and northern two-thirds of the U.S.

Blue grosbeak
Guiraca caerulea

A LTHOUGH THE blue grosbeak, which is not a resident of northern and western forests like many of its close relatives, will become a regular feeder visitor, its primary spring-through-fall diet includes a wide array of insects and spiders. Most members of this species spend the winter months south of the United States, although milder winters will find more of them remaining resident. The growing availability of feeders throughout their range has encouraged this adaptation.

The blue grosbeak particularly enjoys the security of hedgerows, thickets, brush piles and dense patches of weeds. It is commonly spotted in such locations, both in close proximity to people and quite distant from human habitation. Vacant lots and former farmlands allowed to revert to weedy areas also are hugely attractive to the species.

Breeds throughout southern half of the U.S., further north along the Atlantic Coast. Winters in Central America.

The blue grosbeak lays three to five white or pale blue eggs in a deep hair-, rootlet- and grass-lined cup woven from grass, leaves, weed stems, bark strips and snakeskins. The nest is usually in a tree, shrub or tangle of vines 3 to 8 feet (1-2.5m) off the ground.

Rose-breasted grosbeak

Pheucticus ludovicianus

Spotter's Checklist

Plumage
Black head, black wings and tail with white patches, rose breast, white sides and belly. Female streaked brown and white with white eyebrow.

Bill
Large, cone-shaped, silver.

Feet
Anisodactyl, reddish gray.

Body length
About 8 inches (20cm).

Size

Habitat
Woodlands, fields with shrubs, old orchards.

Food
Fruits, seeds, insects and spiders; fruit blossoms in spring. At the feeder, oil-type sunflower seeds.

Song
"Cheer-e-ly, cheer-ip, cheer-e-ly;" also a series of whistles that slur together; also an occasional "chink."

The rose-breasted grosbeak lays three to six gray, green or blue eggs, spotted and blotched with brown and purple, in a cup very loosely woven from twigs and weed stems. The nest is usually placed in the fork of a deciduous tree or shrub 6 to 25 feet (1.8-7.6m) off the ground.

ALTHOUGH THE rose-breasted grosbeak is not an uncommon bird throughout its range in northeastern North America, it spends much of its time in the treetops and therefore is often not recognized by many backyard birders. Further, much of the North American population migrates south of the U.S. border for the winter; this also eliminates the possibility of sightings, since most feeders are stocked only during the colder months. Birdbaths, however, will bring both seasonal residents and migrants in for closer viewing.

The bird's large, powerful bill obviously enables it to eat all the seeds it wants, but the rose-breasted grosbeak prefers fruits and fruit tree blossoms. It also eats a large number of insects. Some estimates place the proportion of insects to fruit at almost 50-50.

The male and female share nest-building, brooding and rearing duties. The pair will produce two broods each year across all but the most northerly extent of the species' range. The male will take responsibility for tending the first batch of fledglings, while the female sits on the second clutch of eggs.

Breeds from central Canada south through the central U.S. and the Appalachians.

Red crossbill

Loxia curvirostra

THE RED crossbill carries one of the strangest bills of all our backyard birds. The mandibles are crossed at the tips, an arrangement that allows the bird to open its primary food source, pine cones, to extract the seeds inside. Holding the cone with a foot, the bird jams its closed bill under the scale of the cone and opens its bill to pry the scale open. It then plucks the seed with its tongue. The crossed bill seems to develop after the young birds leave the nest.

As with many finch species, failure of the seed crop in its native forests of central Canada and the western United States is the factor that usually determines if backyards across the rest of the continent will see many, few or none of the birds during the winter. During these movements, properties planted with mature pine and spruce trees are most likely to draw the birds' attention. They will also frequent feeders stocked with sunflower and niger seeds. Pine cones can be a special treat. When they find a constant source of food they tend to set up residence for the season nearby. It is a trusting bird that generally allows close approach.

Breeds from Alaska and central Canada south and east throughout the western U.S. and along the Appalachians in the east. Winters throughout that range and south to Mexico.

The red crossbill lays three to five pale, blue- or green-white eggs, spotted with brown and purple, in a moss-, grass-, feather- and fur-lined nest, loosely massed of twigs, wood and bark strips. The nest is usually on a coniferous branch 5 to 80 feet (1.5-24.5m) off the ground.

Dickcissel
Spiza americana

Emberizids: Emberizidae

Spotter's Checklist

Plumage
Gray with cream eyebrows, cheek bars and chin; red-brown shoulder patch, cream breast with black "V." Female similar but duller.

Bill
Short, stout, blue-gray.

Feet
Anisodactyl, gray.

Body length
About 6 inches (15cm).

Size

Habitat
Agricultural areas with grain fields and weedy areas.

Food
Seeds, grains, insects and spiders. At the feeder, oil-type sunflower seeds and cracked corn.

Song
"Dick-dick-sissel" repeated many times from an elevated perch.

The dickcissel lays three to five pale blue eggs in a grass-, rootlet- and hair-lined cup woven loosely into the surrounding vegetation. Made from weed stems, grass and leaves, the nest is usually placed on or close to the ground in heavy vegetation.

TODAY A resident primarily of the central United States, the dickcissel, once commonly inhabited a much larger range that extended east as far as the Atlantic Ocean coastal plain. However, in recent years the species has been reestablishing itself in much of the territory it abandoned in the mid-nineteenth century. In addition, some fall migrants turn up east of its primary range — and some to the west — each year.

These birds will establish themselves as winter residents in areas where backyard birders offer cracked corn, grains and sunflower seeds directly on the ground, and thick brush piles can be located for overnight roosting. Most of the population, however, moves south of the U.S. border. During these migrations flocks of hundreds of the birds may turn up in backyards all along the migration route.

At all times during the year and in its various movements, the dickcissel favors open agricultural areas with ample weed patches. During the period of the year when farmlands are inactive, it frequents properties that offer plots of weeds. Breeds throughout the central U.S.

Indigo bunting
Passerina cyanea

The indigo bunting lays two to six pale blue-white eggs in a grass-, hair- and feather-lined cup woven from grass, strips of bark, weed stems and twigs. The nest is usually placed in the crotch of a shrub or tangle of vines 2 to 12 feet (0.6-3.6m) off the ground.

YOU'D BE hard pressed to find a deeper blue on any North American bird than that of the male indigo bunting. However, the appearance of the bird is not caused by its coloration but by the construction of each of its feather barbs. This special structure bends light rays passing through it in such a way that only the blue wavelengths are not scattered. The true color of the bird's plumage, which can be deciphered from certain angles, is actually a dark brown.

Second growth areas, which predominate in much of suburban America, are the favored habitat of the indigo bunting. Treelines with shrubs are ideal.

Nearly the entire population winters in Central America, so the indigo bunting is not a feeder bird. It will, however, establish its courtship and nesting territory in backyards that provide suitable habitat. Each male's territory generally borders on that of another male, and the neighbors appear to recognize one another's songs. In addition, the songs of neighboring males become quite similar as the less dominant birds come to imitate their more dominant neighbors. In this manner they gain protection from the reputation that the more dominant bird has won through skirmishes with other males. Breeds throughout eastern half of U.S. and southern Canada.

Spotter's Checklist

Plumage
Bright blue with black on wings, tail and rump. Female gray-brown above, streaked gray and off-white below.

Bill
Large, cone-shaped, black.

Feet
Anisodactyl, dark gray.

Body length
About 5½ inches (14cm).

Size

Habitat
Brushy areas, old agricultural areas, woodland edges.

Food
Almost exclusively insects and spiders in summer; seeds and fruit. Not much of a feeder bird.

Song
"Tea, to-you, to-you, chew, tea, tea, to-you, to-you."

Painted bunting
Passerina ciris

The painted bunting lays three to five blue- or gray-white eggs, spotted with red-brown, in a grass-, rootlet- and hair-lined cup woven from leaves, grass and weed stems. The nest is usually attached quite firmly to twigs 3 to 14 feet (1-4.2m) off the ground, sometimes in clusters of Spanish moss.

DESPITE THE bright colors of the male in breeding plumage, the painted bunting is not easily seen. It is a shy bird which prefers to remain in dense thickets and hedgerows, and darts off at the slightest disruption. Only during the courtship period is it easy to locate, when the male spends hours on end singing from atop a conspicuous perch. At other times would-be viewers more often than not must content themselves with catching a note or two from a hidden bird.

Much of the population winters south of the U.S. border, but significant numbers of the birds spend the winter months in the Gulf Coast states. There they are readily attracted to backyard feeders and bird baths that are placed close to thick escape cover.

Also commonly referred to as the nonpareil, which translates to "without equal," the painted bunting is a common resident of much of the southern United States. The male's bright plumage made the species a target of cagebird collectors until such use of native species was made illegal. These remain a threat to the species at the southerly extent of its annual migration. Breeds throughout the southeastern U.S.

Brown towhee

Pipilo fuscus

THE BROWN towhee exists in two distinct populations, neither of which migrates or otherwise affords opportunity for mingling and mixing. One population exists in the Pacific coastal states, while the other resides from Texas north to southern Colorado and west through New Mexico and Arizona. Although there are slight differences in coloration between the two populations, there is equal variation of the birds within each population. The Pacific population replaces the traditional towhee-type call with a "chip-chip-chip." And the two populations demonstrate distinctly different preferences in habitat. The coastal population is readily found in backyards and parks, while the landlocked population is more at home in scrubby, mountain areas.

The brown towhee is a real homebody in those locations where its daily needs are met. The entire family may take up residence year-round. A weed patch allowed to go to seed and remain throughout the year, and bird baths close to cover, improve the chances of this taking place.

Resident throughout California and southwestern U.S. east into Texas.

Plumage
Chocolate to gray-brown above, off-white to buff below, yellow throat streaked brown.

Bill
Conical, black.

Feet
Anisodactyl, dark gray.

Body length
About 8½ inches (21 cm).

Size

Habitat
Brushy, weedy areas.

Food
Seeds, fruits and berries, and insects and spiders. At the feeder, proso millets and cracked corn.

Song
"Drink-ya-tea, drink-ya-tea."

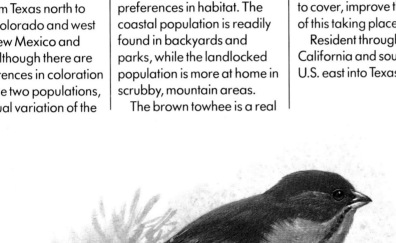

The brown towhee lays three or four blue-green to brownish white eggs spotted with dark brown in a grass- and hair-lined cup of twigs, leaves, grass and weed stems. The nest is usually less than 10 feet (3m) off the ground in a small tree or shrub.

Rufous-sided towhee

Pipilo erythrophthalmus

THE HANDSOMELY colored rufous-sided towhee is a joy to watch as it bounces about the leaf matter under a hedge or in a thicket, or simply on the forest floor, kicking leaves into the air in its constant search for insects, seeds and berries. They have a distinctive approach to this rummaging through the leaves: kicking with both feet at the same time. In the process, the bird creates a disproportionate amount of noise for its size. Hearing without seeing one in the forest readies the listener for the approach of a much larger creature.

Although the song and call of the species varies across its range about as much as any bird, the entire species was named for the call of some individuals that naturalist Mark Catesby encountered in 1731 in the Carolinas. There is equal variety of appearance, with a white-eyed population in the southeastern U.S. and a western population that sports a white-spotted back. Until recently, these differences had led the ornithological community to believe the different populations to be distinct species. They were later officially classified as the red-eyed towhee, white-eyed towhee and spotted towhee.

Breeds from southern Canada south throughout all but Great Plains of the U.S. Winters north as far as Maryland and British Columbia.

The rufous-sided towhee lays three to six gray-white eggs spotted with red-brown, usually more heavily at the large end. The nest is a grass-, hair- and pine needle-lined, loose structure of weed stems, twigs, leaves, grass and bark strips, usually on the ground or in a shrub no more than 5 feet (1.5m) off the ground.

Chipping sparrow
Spizella passerina

THE FEMALE chipping sparrow is so ardent in her quest for even more hair with which to line her nest that previous generations dubbed the species as the "hair bird." Horsehair was the preferred building material when horses were common on farms across the country, but with the move to machinery in agriculture the chipping sparrow has broadened its tastes. The female has not, however, lost her ambitions to garner as much of the material as possible. Sleeping dogs and humans are common targets of her plucking.

The chipping sparrow, which today is a resident of nearly all of North America, has benefited greatly from the settlement of the continent. They previously existed primarily in forest clearings and at woodland edges, but have adapted to the similar type of habitat provided by suburban development and greatly expanded their range.

Commonly sharing the nickname of "chippie" with the chipmunk, the chipping sparrow is a common backyard bird across its substantial range. It is not attracted to feeders, but plantings of conifers and evergreen shrubs provide the preferred nesting locations.

Breeds from all but northern Canada south through all but southern U.S. Winters as far north as Maryland and southern California.

The chipping sparrow lays two to five blue-green eggs, spotted and blotched with black, brown and purple. The hair- and grass-lined nest is woven from grass, weed stems and rootlets. It is usually placed in a coniferous tree or shrub, or vine, as much as 25 feet (7.6m) off the ground and sometimes on the ground.

Spotter's Checklist

Plumage
Gray face with red-brown cap and black line through eye, streaked tan and black on back, wings and tail, off-white underside.

Bill
Short, sharp, black.

Feet
Anisodactyl, pinkish.

Body length
About 5¼ inches (13cm).

Size

Habitat
Brushy areas, open grassy areas, woodland edges.

Food
Small seeds and insects and spiders. At the feeder, oil-type sunflower seeds and cracked corn.

Song
Rapid trill.

Song sparrow

Meliospiza melodia

THE SONG sparrow is one of North America's most common bird species, found nearly everywhere on the continent. However, it is also a widely varied species, ranging from large, dark birds in Alaska's Aleutian Islands to much smaller, lighter birds in the southwestern United States. The song also has been found to vary across the bird's range, with more than a dozen different regional dialects. To complicate matters further, each individual male is estimated to be capable of nearly a thousand variations on a repertoire of as many as 20 basic song patterns. The basic structure of song is instinctive in each bird, but it develops its full repertoire by hearing, matching and then individualizing the songs of other birds it hears.

Thick cover, such as hedgerows, thickets and dense patches of weeds, enhances the appeal of any backyard for the song sparrow. This is particularly true during the breeding season, when the birds insist on such locations to place their nests. Visits to feeders can be encouraged by placing them near such cover. The bird prefers to feed on the ground on low feeding platforms.

Breeds from southern Alaska and central Canada south through the northern U.S. and to U.S.-Mexican border in the west. Breeds throughout the U.S. and north along the Pacific Coast into Alaska.

The song sparrow lays three to six green-white eggs, spotted and blotched with red-brown and purple. The grass-, rootlet- and hair-lined cup is woven from grass, weed stems, leaves and strips of bark. The nest is usually placed either on the ground in a cluster of weeds or a brush pile, or as much as 12 feet (3.6m) off the ground in a shrub or tree.

Field sparrow

Spizella pusilla

Spotter's Checklist

Plumage
Gray face, red-brown cap, white eyering, streaked tan, dark brown and slate along back and wings, buff underside.

Bill
Short, stout, pink.

Feet
Anisodactyl, bright pink.

Body length
About 5¼ inches (13cm).

Size

Habitat
Reverting agricultural areas.

Food
Seeds and fruits and berries; some insects and spiders. At the feeder, oil-type sunflower and niger seeds.

Song
Rapid whistle, ending in a trill.

WEEDY AREAS are the preferred habitat of the field sparrow, which has rapidly expanded its range over the past few decades as more farmlands have been left to fall into disuse. However, as these same locations now succeed back into woodlands, the numbers of birds living there are dwindling. This does not mean that the population as a whole is threatened. Suburban development provides plenty of this type of habitat on an ongoing basis.

Like the chipping sparrow, the field sparrow prefers to line its nest with animal hair. This need provides a means of attracting the bird to nest in the backyard by offering a mesh bag filled with animal and human hair. The bag should be placed so that the hair can be taken from a perched position, as the field sparrow cannot hover while plucking the hair.

Some of the population, particularly those birds in northernmost U.S. and southern Canada, migrate short distances to the south each fall. But most field sparrows are permanent residents of the areas where they nest.

Breeds throughout eastern half of the U.S. Winters as far north as Pennsylvania and Nebraska.

The field sparrow lays two to five blue- or green-white eggs spotted with red-brown and purple. The grass-, rootlet- and hair-lined cup is woven from weed stems, grass, and leaves. The nest is usually placed either on the ground or as much as 4 feet (1.2m) off the ground in dense shrub or a tree.

House sparrow

Passer domesticus

Spotter's Checklist

Plumage
Gray cheek, breast, sides and belly; patterned black and tan on wings and tail; red-brown cap; black throat. Female and young are duller and lack black throat.

Bill
Short, stout, tan or cream.

Feet
Anisodactyl, gray.

Body length
About 6 inches (15cm).

Size

Habitat
Residential areas, agricultural areas.

Food
Seeds, fruits and berries, insects and spiders. At the feeder, cracked corn, sunflower seeds.

Song
Repeated chirps, lacking any true musical qualities.

The house sparrow lays three to seven off-white eggs spotted with gray and brown in a mass of grass, weeds, feathers and debris in any type of cavity.

THIS NATIVE of Europe, Asia and Africa was unknown in the wild on the North American continent until 1850, when a handful of the birds were released into Central Park in New York City. They found the largely unoccupied ecological niche of life in close proximity to humanity in its towns and cities to their liking and rapidly multiplied. From those first few birds, we now have house sparrows everywhere throughout the United States and the southern half of Canada.

The species continues to reside only where humans live. The birds commonly build their nests in manmade structures, such as flower pots and pairs of pants hanging on washlines. They also are drawn to natural cavities, which has placed them in competition with the eastern bluebird to the detriment of this native species. Although habitat loss was the primary factor leading to substantial declines in the bluebird population in earlier decades of this century, competition from the aggressive immigrant also took its toll. The house sparrow has become an agricultural pest in some locations. Resident from central Canada south throughout the U.S.

White-throated sparrow
Zonotrichia albicollis

Plumage
Streaked tan and black across back and wings, head striped black and white, gray breast and belly, white throat. Female and young are duller.

Bill
Short, sharp, dark gray.

Feet
Anisodactyl, pinkish brown.

Body length
About 6½ inches (16cm).

Size

Habitat
Coniferous woodlands, brushy areas; residential areas in winter.

Food
Seeds and insects and spiders. At the feeder, oil-type sunflower seeds.

Song
"Tooo, ti-ti-ti, teee, ti-ti-ti, ti-ti-ti, ti-ti-ti."

THE LILTING song of the white-throated sparrow just might be the most commonly recognized among the sparrow family, although the bird is far from our most widespread or common sparrow species. However, the population spreads out across much of the United States on its annual fall migration south from its breeding grounds in northern Canada, and the male begins his courtship song long before returning north in the spring.

The white-throated sparrow is one of the backyard species that you can rely upon as a regular feeder visitor. Just about any feeding arrangement is to the bird's liking, as long as it is on or near ground level. Flocks will set themselves up in backyards that provide a constant supply of food with thick cover such as hedgerows, thickets and brush piles, and remain there throughout the winter. They will gather in these areas of cover as night falls, uttering their metallic flocking call. The white-throated sparrow is also an avid bather, eager for water on even the coldest day.

Breeds from central Canada south through the Great Lakes region and Pennsylvania. Winters throughout eastern U.S.

The white-throated sparrow lays three to six tan or green-white eggs spotted and blotched with red-brown. The grass-, rootlet- and hair-lined cup is woven from grass, rootlets, twigs, pine needles and strips of bark. The nest is usually placed either on the ground in a cluster of weeds or brush pile, or occasionally as much as 3 feet (1m) off the ground in a thick shrub.

White-crowned sparrow
Zonotrichia leucophrys

The white-crowned sparrow lays three to five pale blue eggs blotched with darker areas in a cup of fine grasses on or close to the ground.

IN THE eastern half of North America, the white-crowned sparrow is much less common than the similar white-throated sparrow. However, in many flocks of mostly white-throated birds a few white-crowned sparrows can be found. The latter is more slender than the former, lacks the yellow spot between eye and bill, and generally stands more erect.

A great deal of our early knowledge into the physical aspects of bird migration came from the white-crowned sparrow, which was widely used in laboratory experiments. Much of the species' population undertakes a fall migration from the breeding grounds in northern Canada and Alaska into the southern two-thirds of the United States.

The white-crowned sparrow is one of those species that can be quickly conditioned to accept food directly from human hands. Like its white-throated cousin, it can be coaxed into easy view by making a squeaking noise, which usually causes the bird to alight on top of the nearest bush to investigate the source of the sound. Otherwise, it spends most of its time feeding on the ground.

Breeds from Alaska and northern Canada south through the Rockies and along the Atlantic Coast. Winters throughout southern U.S. as far north as British Columbia and New Jersey.

Savannah sparrow

Passerculus sandwichensis

THE SAVANNAH sparrow is the most common of the grassland sparrows, spending most of its time in fields, prairies and grass-covered dunes. When startled, it chooses to drop into the grass and run away rather than take flight. The species cannot be considered a regular feeder visitor, but birds will come to feeding stations in severe weather. Allowing a patch of weeds to go to seed and remain standing through the winter definitely serves to attract the birds. A nearby brush pile enhances the appeal of such a setting by providing a quick escape route. The savannah sparrow is commonly seen in the backyard and areas of human habitation during its fall migration, when huge flocks descend upon any likely site for a brief respite.

Nearly 20 races of the species have been recognized across its wide and varied range. Some, like the large and pale Ipswich sparrow of the Nova Scotia coastline, were considered separate species until recently. Another race, this on the West Coast, also might appear to be a totally different species, with its rich chocolate-brown plumage.

Breeds throughout Alaska and Canada south to New Jersey and Mexico. Winters as far north as New England and southern Alaska.

The savannah sparrow lays three to six off-white eggs heavily spotted and blotched with brown (more heavily at the large end), in a grass-, rootlet- and hair-lined circle of larger grasses. The nest is usually placed in a hollow on the ground among and under thick vegetation.

Spotter's Checklist

Plumage
Streaked tan, gray and black, bright yellow eyebrows.

Bill
Short, sharp, gray over yellow.

Feet
Anisodactyl, gray.

Body length
About 5¼ inches (13cm).

Size

Habitat
Agricultural areas, prairies, grasslands.

Food
Seeds and insects and spiders. Visits feeders only during periods of extreme weather.

Song
"Tsip-tsip-tsip-tseeee-rrr."

Dark-eyed junco

Junco hyemalis

Spotter's Checklist

Plumage
Gray to gray-brown above, white belly and underside of tail.

Bill
Short, rounded, pink.

Feet
Anisodactyl, gray.

Body length
About 5¾ inches (13cm).

Size

Habitat
Woodlands; residential and agricultural areas.

Food
Seeds in winter; mostly insects and spiders in summer. At the feeder, niger seeds, cracked corn, proso millets.

Song
Burry trill, sometimes with a bell-like tone.

THE DARK-eyed junco is another species whose wide regional variations in color and size have given rise to many different names. For example, the slate-colored junco of the east, the black-headed Oregon junco of the west and the white-winged junco of South Dakota all were considered separate species at one time. However, they interbreed freely wherever their ranges intersect and are now defined as variations on the same species.

Regardless of its coloring or local name, the dark-eyed junco is one of the most dependable and predictable feeder birds. Flocks will appear at the first signals of winter's approach. They may disappear during periods of mild, clear weather but will be right back at the feeder just as soon as the next approaching winter storm is detected. Nearly any of the common feeder seeds are acceptable to the birds, which prefer to feed at ground level or on a low feeding table. Nearby

escape cover, such as a hedgerow or a brush pile, and a few coniferous trees or tall shrubs for night roosting greatly enhance the appeal of any backyard.

Breeds from Alaska and all but northern Canada south through the northern U.S. and further along the Appalachians and Pacific Coast. Winters throughout the U.S. and southern Canada.

The dark-eyed junco lays three to six blue-white eggs, heavily spotted and blotched with red-brown and purple at the large end. The grass-, rootlet- and hair-lined bowl of grass, rootlets, twigs, strips of bark and moss is usually placed on the ground along a ledge, among tree roots, under or in a log, occasionally as much as 8 feet (2.4m) above the ground.

Black-capped chickadee

Parus atricapillus

YOU CAN almost set your watch by the regular appearances of flocks of black-capped chickadees at the backyard feeder throughout the winter. These small balls of energy establish their daily rounds of feeders in a given neighborhood and stick to that schedule with a fair amount of regularity for the rest of the season, so long as the feeders continue to offer seed. (Suet and peanut butter also are relished.) The black-capped chickadee is another of the species that can be readily trained to take food out of your hand.

The traveling flocks might also include creepers, nuthatches, kinglets and small woodpeckers, although such mixed flocks are more common in woodland settings. The flocks disband in late winter and early spring, but individual pairs of black-capped chickadees can be encouraged to remain in the backyard for nesting by placing nest boxes at the edges of wooded areas. Only properties with mature trees will be used for nesting. Although the species is generally a permanent resident, large migrations do occur in some falls. At these times much larger flocks will be seen than those that frequent feeders during the winter.

Breeds from Alaska and central Canada south through the northern half of the U.S. Winters throughout the same range but also a bit further south.

The black-capped chickadee lays five to ten white eggs spotted with red-brown, more heavily at the large end, in a cavity filled with a bundle of hair, fur, moss, feathers, wool and similar materials. The bird often carves the cavity itself from soft, rotting wood, but also uses existing cavities.

Spotter's Checklist

Plumage
Black cap and chin, white cheek stripe, gray shoulders and back, gray wing feathers edged with white, buff breast and belly.

Bill
Short, sharp, black.

Feet
Anisodactyl, dark gray.

Body length
About 5¼ inches (13cm).

Size

Habitat
Woodlands; residential areas in winter.

Food
Seeds and fruits and berries in winter; mostly insects and spiders in summer. At the feeder, oil-type sunflower seeds, suet and peanut butter.

Song
"Fee-bee-bee;" also a series of high-pitched, stuttered notes.

Carolina chickadee
Parus carolinensis

Spotter's Checklist

Plumage
Similar to black-capped chickadee but wing feathers show less white edging.

Bill
Short, sharp, black.

Feet
Anisodactyl, dark gray.

Body length
About 4½ inches (11cm).

Size

Habitat
Woodlands, residential areas.

Food
Mostly insects and spiders, but also seeds and fruits and berries. At the feeder, sunflower seeds, suet, peanut butter.

Song
"Fee-bee-bee-bee;" also a series of high-pitched, stuttered notes.

THE CAROLINA chickadee is the source of much confusion with the black-capped chickadee. The ranges of the two birds overlap very slightly and only in the Appalachian Mountains: the Carolina chickadee to the south and the black-capped to the north. In the small zone where their ranges do overlap, the Carolina chickadee generally keeps to lower elevations than the black-capped. It was Audubon who discovered the differences in 1834, more than a century after Europeans had first documented the chickadee as a species.

The southern bird shares its northern cousin's love for the backyard feeder and fills much the same niche in its environment. Like the black-capped chickadee, it is often found in mixed flocks with creepers, nuthatches, kinglets and small woodpeckers. The same techniques can be used to attract either species, both in the winter and for spring and summer nesting.

A flock of Carolina chickadees is usually made up of members of the same family who are quick to detect outsiders. They tend to occupy the same territory throughout many generations. They are short-lived birds, and share great similarities in their song patterns. Resident from New Jersey and Ohio south through the Gulf states.

The Carolina chickadee lays five to eight white eggs spotted with red-brown, more heavily at the large end, in a cavity filled with a cluster of hair, fur, feathers, moss, ferns and plant down (particularly thistle). The bird usually excavates its cavity in a rotting tree stump from 4 to 6 feet (1.2-1.8m) off the ground.

Carolina wren

Thryothorus ludovicianus

THE CAROLINA wren is not an annual migrant, tending to remain resident in its own territory. However, severe winters with heavy snows in the northern extent of the species' range, have had a double-edged impact, forcing many of the birds to move temporarily to the south and killing many more that refuse to leave.

The Carolina wren is a ground forager, eating primarily insects and spiders, and under such harsh weather conditions its source of food quickly vanishes. It will supplement its winter diet with oil-type sunflower seed from the feeder, but much prefers suet and peanut butter. Water is another attractive backyard feature throughout the winter, and loose brush piles are certain to attract any wrens in the vicinity. The species readily accepts nearly any opening, from pockets in pants hung on the washline to mailboxes to discarded tin cans, as substitutes for its more natural nesting sites such as tree stumps to leaf litter. The birds also readily accept small nest boxes, particularly when they are placed near brush piles, hedgerows or thickets.

Found throughout eastern U.S. as far north as the Great Lakes and New England.

The Carolina wren lays four to eight pinkish white eggs heavily spotted with brown, particularly at the larger end, in a cavity filled with a hair-, moss-, grass- and feather-lined mass of twigs, leaves, moss, weed stems, strips of bark and debris. The cavity has a side entrance, and is usually as much as 10 feet (3m) off the ground.

Spotter's Checklist

Plumage
Warm brown above, buff below, white line above each eye running to back of head and curving downward.

Bill
Long, sharp, gray.

Feet
Anisodactyl, silvery gray.

Body length
About 5½ inches (14cm).

Size

Habitat
Brushy woodlands, brushy fields.

Food
Mostly insects and spiders; seeds in winter. At the feeder, suet, peanut butter and some oil-type sunflower seeds.

Song
"Wee-kettle, wee-kettle, wee-kettle."

House wren
Troglodytes aedon

Spotter's Checklist

Plumage
Gray-brown above, darker speckling on head, darker stripes on wings and tail, buff to gray breast and underside.

Bill
Long, sharp, dark gray, slight downward curve.

Feet
Anisodactyl, light brown.

Body length
About 5 inches (13cm).

Size

Habitat
Woodland edges, agricultural areas, residential areas.

Food
Almost exclusively insects and spiders. At the feeder, suet and peanut butter.

Song
Bubbling and bursting, rising and falling.

The house wren lays five to eight eggs speckled with many small red-brown spots in a cup of grass, weed stems, rootlets, hair, feathers and debris. The female builds this cup in a cavity where the male has placed an incomplete nest of twigs, or on her own bed of twigs.

WHILE THE ordinary brown plumage of the house wren makes it a rather undecorative bird for the backyard, the species' nesting habits more than make up for that shortcoming in the eyes of many backyard birders. These small birds are among the most eager-beavers of all our bird species in their near-constant pursuit of nesting sites. They readily accept nearly any nest box, regardless of dimension or description, and will fill every nest box they find in their territory with "dummy" nests.

They will reuse old nests, but not before they completely dismantle and reassemble them piece by piece. No opening is safe from their quest for additional nesting sites. Everything from pockets in laundry on the washline to mailboxes to drain pipes to sun-bleached animal skulls have been reported as providing their nesting cavities.

One habit of the house wren that does not add to its otherwise endearing nature is its penchant for invading the nests of other birds in the area and piercing their eggs with its bill. The species' diet is almost exclusively insects and spiders. It generally migrates southward before the feeder season. However, when the birds do spend their winters further north, they readily accept suet and peanut butter.

Breeds throughout southern Canada and the U.S., except for the Deep South. Winters as far north as the Carolinas and southern Canada.

Winter wren
Troglodytes troglodytes

THE WINTER wren is a secretive little bird most at home picking its way among the dense undergrowth along the banks of a woodland stream or some mountain forest. Few things the backyard birder does will attract the species. Insects and spiders provide nearly all of the bird's diet, only occasionally supplemented with seeds of wild plants. The winter wren prefers to build a domed nest on or near the ground, so nest boxes have no drawing power. Only long-standing, well-weathered brush piles amid dense undergrowth seem to have any special drawing power on the bird. Occasionally a passing individual will take advantage of suet.

Because of the species' skulking nature it is often difficult to spot the bird, even when it's common in the area. However, the loud, bubbling quality of its song offers unmistakable evidence of its presence.

The male mates with several different females, each one of which will build its own nest within his territory. However he shares in the rearing responsibility for each group of nestlings because mating takes place at spaced intervals.

Breeds all along Pacific Coast, throughout central and southeastern Canada and south along the Appalachians. Winters along Pacific Coast and throughout eastern half of U.S.

The winter wren lays four to seven white eggs spotted with red-brown in a hair- and feather-lined mass of grass, weed stems, twigs, moss, and rootlets in the roots of a fallen tree, cavity or crevice.

White-breasted nuthatch
Sitta carolinensis

L OOK TO the origins of the nuthatch's common name and you will gain great insight into the nuthatch's habits. The first European settlers to encounter the bird dubbed it the "nuthack" for its habit of jamming nuts into the crevice of a tree and hacking away at them with its bill until they crack open. This habit has endeared them to many backyard birders, who enjoy their constant trips from feeder to tree carrying one seed each time.

Their special approach to feeding on the sides of trees is equally captivating. Like many bark-gleaning birds, such as woodpeckers and chickadees, the nuthatch moves along the side of the tree searching in the cracks of the bark for insects. But, while most bark-gleaners move up the tree, the nuthatch moves down the tree headfirst. In this manner the nuthatch spots morsels that the other birds have missed.

This specialized feeding mechanism allows the nuthatch to utilize the same feeding spots as the other birds but in a different manner and provides part of the explanation for the mixed flocks of nuthatches, chickadees, creepers, kinglets and small woodpeckers that are common throughout the winter woodlands.

Resident throughout western and eastern U.S. and Canada, absent only from the central U.S.

The white-breasted nuthatch lays ten pinkish white eggs spotted with brown and lilac in a mass of grass, twigs, rootlets, hair, fur and strips of bark in a cavity 10 to 50 feet (3-15m) off the ground.

Red-breasted nuthatch
Sitta canadensis

THE RED-breasted nuthatch shares nearly all of the characteristics described for its white-breasted cousin, but shows a decided liking for coniferous trees and the seeds of pine cones. It also focuses its feeding attention more to the outer branches of trees than the trunk-hugging white-breasted nuthatch.

When the two species occur together, the red-breasted is easily differentiated by this habit and by the black-and-white stripes running across its head and face from bill to neck and its reddish brown breast. Numbers of red-breasted nuthatches will vary substantially from one year to the next. The conifer seed crop is the determining factor, and when it fails the northern populations of the birds fly south. Many of these migrants can be encouraged to remain for the nesting season by providing nesting boxes, particularly if covered with pine bark. The red-breasted nuthatch is less of a feeder bird than the white-breasted variety, and is more readily attracted to properties with mature conifers. Suet offered on the trunk of a tree is a favored food.

Breeds from central Canada south throughout the western U.S., northeastern U.S. and along the Appalachians.

The red-breasted nuthatch lays four to seven white eggs, heavily spotted with red-brown, in a loose mat of grass, strips of bark, moss and feathers in a cavity 5 to 40 feet (1.5-12m) off the ground. The entrance hole always shows a smear of pine resin that the birds apply there.

Brown creeper
Certhia americana

Spotter's Checklist

Plumage
Mottled tan, brown and black above with streaking of white on cap; gray eyebrows, chin, breast and underside.

Bill
Long, pointed, brown with white at mandible edges.

Feet
Anisodactyl, gray.

Body length
About 5½ inches (14cm).

Size

Habitat
Woodlands; residential areas in winter.

Food
Mostly insects and spiders. Not much of a feeder bird, but sometimes comes to peanut butter.

Song
"Tsee, tsee, tsee;" also a low warble.

AMONG THE mixed flocks of chickadees, kinglets, nuthatches, small woodpeckers and fellow travellers that cruise the winter woodlands, the brown creeper can easily go unnoticed. It's an inconspicuous little bird, whose streaked brown plumage is overshadowed by the brighter colors of the other members of the mixed flocks. Watch such a flock carefully, however, and you will probably find one or more of these birds.

The brown creeper searches for insects along the trunk of the tree moving upward in a spiraling fashion and, when it reaches the top, it launches and glides to the base of the next tree. It issues its soft call throughout this process. The brown creeper is not an easy bird to attract. It builds its nest on the side of a tree, between the trunk and a loosened bit of bark, and thus has no use for nest boxes.

Its diet is almost entirely insect-based, although passing birds will stop for suet and peanut butter, and then make these locations regular stops during their daily travels. During the fall migration individuals or small groups may turn up just about anywhere along the route.

Breeds from Alaska and central Canada south throughout the western U.S., Great Lakes region and Appalachians. Winters from southern Canada south throughout the U.S.

The brown creeper lays four to eight white eggs spotted with red-brown in a grass-, moss-, and feather-lined platform woven from twigs, bark and leaves beneath a loose bit of bark on the side of a tree. The nest is usually placed 5 to 15 feet (1.5-4.5m) off the ground.

Tufted titmouse
Parus bicolor

THE TUFTED titmouse is another of the feeder visitors that will come to visit the backyard on a near-clockwork schedule. Once a feeder has been found to provide adequate food — particularly peanut hearts and peanut butter — these birds will include it as a part of their year-round territory. Rarely a winter day will pass without their regular visits. They will become quite tame and trusting of humans they encounter regularly along this route.

In the woodland they are often part of the mixed flocks of small birds, but in the backyard generally will be in the company of chickadees. The tufted titmouse is constantly alert to potential danger and usually serves as an early warning system for the other birds in either of these situations. Parent birds seem to introduce their offspring to the best feeding stations each fall. Feeders that are kept stocked into the spring usually will attract the mutual feeding behavior of courting pairs. Until recently the black-crested titmouse of Texas was considered a separate species. Resident throughout the eastern half of the U.S.

The tufted titmouse lays four to eight white eggs spotted with red-brown in a fur-, hair-, and cloth-lined mass of leaves, moss, grass and bark strips in a cavity that may be anywhere from 2 to 87 feet (0.6-26.5m) off the ground.

Plumage
Gray cap, back and wings; white around large black eye, mixed with red-brown along sides and on rump.

Bill
Short, conical, black.

Feet
Anisodactyl, light gray.

Body length
About 6 inches (15cm).

Size

Habitat
Woodlands, residential areas with trees.

Food
Largely insects and spiders, but also seeds and fruits and berries. At the feeder, peanut butter, peanut hearts, suet, oil-type sunflower seeds.

Song
"Here-a, here-a, here-a;" or simply, "here, here, here."

Bushtit
Psaltriparus minimus

Spotter's Checklist

Plumage
Gray above, off-white below, yellow-tan cheek, black-tipped wings and tail.

Bill
Short, conical, black.

Feet
Anisodactyl, black.

Body length
About 4½ inches (11 cm).

Size

Habitat
Wooded areas.

Food
Mostly insects; some seeds and berries. Not a feeder bird.

Song
"Tsip" or "pitt."

Most often bushtits will be observed in small flocks, skittering here and there as a group through the undergrowth of a deciduous or mixed forest. Suddenly they will appear in a whirlwind of jumping, gleaning, scratching and picking, all accompanied by constant group chirping, only to disappear the next moment and then resurface at a new spot a few hundred feet away. Their movement is best described as flowing from one spot to the next

Feeders and nest boxes do not attract them, but neighborhoods that are well planted with mature trees and undergrowth are readily accepted as though they were uninhabited woodlands. If the setting also includes numerous brushpiles and an adequate insect supply, individual pairs may take to nesting when the flocks break up after winter.

Some experts consider several regional variations in the birds to constitute distinct species; among them the black-eared bushtit of New Mexico and Texas, and the lead-colored bushtit of the west. Resident along U.S. Pacific Coast and throughout the southern half of the western U.S.

The bushtit lays five to 15 white eggs in a hanging basket of plant fibers and lichens, with a side entrance near the top. The nest is suspended in a small tree or shrub.

Eastern bluebird
Sialia sialis

N̲O SPECIES of bird better exemplifies the impact that efforts of concerned backyard birders can have than the eastern bluebird. Through the 1940s to the 1970s the population of these birds spiraled swiftly downward. There were several reasons for this decline: changing agricultural practices that eliminated the available snags for nesting sites, competition with introduced species, pesticide poisoning and a few severe winters at disastrously critical points. However, over the past 10 to 15 years, the trend has been reversed by backyard birders, conservation organizations and farmers placing incredible numbers of nest boxes throughout its range.

The bluebird has responded and today can be listed as definitely on the rebound. The species has even become common in some locations. The trend will continue only as long as more property owners erect new boxes. The critical feature of a bluebird nest box is its entrance hole, which must be exactly 1½ inches (38mm) in diameter to prevent use of the box by starlings. In addition, the birds prefer boxes that are located in field-type settings with scattered trees, not closer than 25 feet (7.6m).

Breeds throughout the eastern half of the southern Canada and US. Winters as far north as Pennsylvania and Nebraska.

The eastern bluebird lays three to six pale blue-white eggs in a cavity containing a jumbled mass of coarse grass and weed stems at the center of which is a loosely woven cup of finer grass and weed stems.

Spotter's Checklist

Plumage
Bright blue head, back, wings and tail; red-brown breast fading to off-white underside. Female is duller.

Bill
Short, pointed, brownish.

Feet
Anisodactyl, black.

Body length
About 7 inches (18cm).

Size

Habitat
Fields with scattered trees.

Food
Mostly insects and spiders, but some seeds, fruits and berries. Not much of a feeder bird.

Song
A soft warble of whistles broken by chatter.

Western bluebird
Sialia mexicana

Spotter's Checklist

Plumage
Bluish purple above and on throat, red-brown breast and back, white underside. Female is duller with gray head and throat.

Bill
Long, pointed, black.

Feet
Anisodactyl, black.

Body length
About 7 inches (18cm).

Size

Habitat
Bushy areas, thickets, woodland edges.

Food
Mostly insects and spiders, but some fruits and berries. Not much of a feeder bird.

Song
A soft warble of whistles broken by chatter.

THE WESTERN bluebird, much more a resident of woodlands and deserts, never came under the same types of threats as its eastern cousin and has never undergone similar decline. It also is simply not as selective in its choice of nesting sites and therefore more adaptable in the face of any competition that comes its way. However, even in this area nesting holes can be at a premium and they will readily accept nesting boxes, but they are by no means necessary.

The western bluebird frequents habitats that generally provide stable and adequate food throughout the year and so it is not much of a feeder bird. Properties within its chosen habitats and range can be developed to encourage its frequent stops by planting in a variety of berry-producing plants, particularly mistletoe. The western bluebird is easily differentiated from its eastern cousin by its deeper blue head, bib, back and wings, although the two species have distinctly different ranges and rarely occur in the same location.

Breeds from southwestern Canada south throughout the western third of the U.S. Winters throughout the southern half of the western U.S.

The western bluebird lays four to six light blue eggs in a grass-lined cavity in a small tree or snag.

American robin
Turdus migratorius

THE LONG-standing reputation of the American robin as the ever-reliable harbinger of spring is deeply rooted in American folklore although the truth behind the myth is questionable. Yes, increasing numbers of the familiar red-breasted bird do appear with the warming weather in backyards and fields throughout the northern extent of its range. But these birds are just as likely to have spent the winter in some nearby woodlands as made a migration far to the south. Nevertheless, the robin is probably the most widely recognized bird in North America.

Another special characteristic recognized by nearly every backyard birder is the adult's method of hunting across the lawn for earthworms, insects and spiders. As it moves the bird cocks its head from side to side. It has been widely assumed that the robin was doing this to listen for the sounds of its prey. However, more recently it's been demonstrated that the bird hunts by sight only. Its eyes are fixed in their sockets, so the bird must turn its head to focus on objects at different locations.

Breeds almost continentwide, except for northernmost Canada and southernmost U.S. Winters mostly south of the U.S.-Canadian border, further north along both coasts.

The American robin lays three to five "robin-egg blue" eggs in a deep cup of grass, weed stems, string, cloth and other litter held together with mud. The nest is usually built in the fork of a tree, on a horizontal branch or on a ledge.

Wood thrush

Hylocichla mustelina

Spotter's Checklist

Plumage
Dull brown cap, back of neck, back, wings and tail; white throat, breast and underside with large brown and black spots.

Bill
Long, pointed, gray.

Feet
Anisodactyl, pinkish gray.

Body length
About 8 inches (20cm).

Size

Habitat
Woodlands with lots of brush, brushy residential areas.

Food
Insects, earthworms, berries and seeds. Not a feeder bird.

Song
"EE-o-ay," followed by a fluttering trill.

THE WOOD thrush is the only one of our brown-spotted thrushes that regularly frequents our backyards, even to the point of nesting in those that are well planted with stands of deciduous saplings and thick understory. That thick understory is essential because the bird has retained a highly secretive nature. Luckily for the backyard birder, it also has one of the most beautiful songs of any North American bird. Its flutelike, duetlike quality has inspired many of America's most noted writers on the subjects of natural history and the outdoors.

The wood thrush's diet is primarily insects, worms and spiders, supplemented with berries and seeds, and it generally cannot be attracted to feeders. In addition, nearly the entire population is well south of the U.S. border by winter. However, from spring through fall their strong affinity for water leads the birds to be drawn readily to backyard baths and lawn sprinklers. Because the birds are so commonly observed in swamps and marshes, the nickname of "swamp robin" is commonly given to the species.

Breeds throughout eastern U.S. and southeasternmost Canada. Winters in Central America, although a few birds spend the winter months in Texas and Florida.

The wood thrush lays two to five blue-green eggs in a rootlet-lined cup of leafmold, grass, bark, moss, paper and other litter held together with mud. The nest is usually in the fork of a tree or on a horizontal branch anywhere between 5 to 50 feet (1.5-15m) off the ground.

Hermit thrush
Catharus guttatus

A S ITS common name implies, the hermit thrush is a shy, skulking type of bird most at home in woodlands and swamps. It spends most of its time scratching through the leaf litter and dense undergrowth. A common nickname for the bird is "swamp angel" and, as this implies, the bird carries a near-angelic song that many have compared favorably with even that of the wood thrush. Although the hermit thrush is the only one of our brown-spotted thrushes that regularly winters in the north, it tends to remain in the deep woods and swamps and rarely comes to the feeder. Those that have been observed at feeding stations generally are reported as coming for suet. Plantings of bittersweet, honeysuckle, privet and other such berry-producing plants, in connection with a thick understory, are much more effective measures for attracting the species.

There are many regional variations on the basic coloration of the species, however all seem to have a rust-colored tail that is regularly pumped up and down. In addition, much of the underside will be white with distinct spotting across the bib and breast.

Breeds from Alaska and northwestern Canada south throughout the western U.S. and southeast through northeastern U.S. Most of the population winters along Pacific Coast and throughout the southern third of the U.S.

The hermit thrush lays three or four pale blue eggs. The nest is a bowl loosely made of twigs, strips of bark, grass, moss and ferns and lined with rootlets, plant fibers and conifer needles. It is usually placed on the ground under a low-hanging tree branch or among ferns.

Veery

Catharus fuscescens

The veery lays three to five light blue eggs in a grass- and rootlet-lined cluster of twigs, weed stems and small bits of vine gathered on a pile of dried leaves. The nest is usually placed on the ground, in a brush pile or in a low shrub.

THE VEERY is another species of the deep woods and wooded streamsides that spends most of its time scurrying about through the undergrowth. Nevertheless it is much less shy and wary than most other birds of this description. Properties that possess such features or border on such areas will readily be included in the bird's territory. However, as an insect-, worm- and spider-eater, the veery will not be attracted to any feeder. It has been reported to eat a few berries on occasion, although not enough to suggest that plantings are an effective means of attracting the species.

Wet areas and ground-level baths placed in wooded areas are the most that the backyard birder can do for the veery. Such locations are especially effective during the fall migration, when this species may turn up nearly anywhere along its southerly route. As with many of the thrushes, the song of the veery is exceptionally beautiful. It has been likened to the music of flutes or pan-pipes.

Breeds from southern Canada south through the northern U.S. and further south through the Appalachians and Rockies. Winters in South America.

Blue-gray gnatcatcher

Polioptila caerulea

Spotter's Checklist

Plumage
Light gray cap, back of neck, back, wings and tail with white and black edges on wing and tail feathers; white face, breast and underside.

Bill
Very long, sharp, black, strong downward curve.

Feet
Anisodactyl, black.

Body length
About 3¾ inches (9cm).

Size

Habitat
Woodlands, brushy streamsides.

Food
Exclusively insects and spiders. Not a feeder bird.

Song
A very light warble.

GNATCATCHERS SEEM never to be at rest, flitting from power lines or tree limbs out into midair to snatch yet another flying insect. Looking like a miniature mockingbird, the blue-gray gnatcatcher consumes an incredible number of insects every day, particularly when tending a nest packed with young. Nothing offered at the feeder will attract this species, but a backyard planted with mature trees that attract plenty of insects may draw it in. The blue-gray gnatcatcher may chose to build its nest in such a setting, a structure woven of plant down held together by spider cobwebs and covered with bits of

lichens. Generally it is located high in a tree and near water. Parents tending to nestlings will be even more active than normal. At such times the birds seem unconcerned about the approach of any intruders.

Breeds from northern California, Great Lakes and southeastern Canada south through the U.S. Winters as far north as southern California and the Carolinas.

The blue-gray gnatcatcher lays four or five blue-white to brown eggs with dark spots in a bark- and plant down-lined cup. This is tightly woven from oak catkins, plant down, strips from weed stems held together with spider and insect silk and covered with bits of lichen. The nest is securely fastened to a tree limb or small fork of a tree anywhere from 5 to 70 feet (1.5-21.3m) off the ground.

Golden-crowned kinglet
Regulus satrapa

Plumage
Green-brown above, lighter below, white eyebrows, orange crown edged with yellow, two off-white wing bars. Female and young have solid yellow cap.

Bill
Short, pointed, black.

Feet
Anisodactyl, dark reddish brown.

Body length
About 3¾ inches (9cm).

Size

Habitat
Coniferous woodlands; deciduous woodlands and thickets in winter.

Food
Insects and spiders; some berries in winter. At the feeder, suet and peanut butter.

Song
"Ti-ti-ti" followed by chattering.

The golden-crowned kinglet lays five to ten off-white eggs spotted or blotched with brown and gray in a hanging mass of moss and lichen lined with rootlets, bark strips and feathers. The nest is woven into the twigs of a horizontal branch of a conifer from 5 to 60 feet (1.5-18.3m) off the ground.

LIKE MANY predators, the golden-crowned kinglet's population seems to be governed by a primary prey species. In the case of the kinglet, this prey species seems to be the spruce bud worm. When the insect is plentiful during the summer, much larger numbers of the kinglets seem to appear on the wintering grounds to the south the following fall.

The golden-crowned kinglet is one of those species that make up the mixed flocks of chickadees, creepers, kinglets, small woodpeckers and titmice that roam the winter woods. The kinglet prefers coniferous woodlands, although the species spreads out into mixed and deciduous woodlands during the winter.

Their diet is primarily insects, and they are quite skilled at locating hibernating insects in bark crevices. They are attracted to feeders only during the most severe weather, and then mostly to suet and peanut butter. Backyards planted with conifers are attractive to the birds, particularly if they are densely packed together and include spruce.

Breeds from Alaska and western Canada south throughout the western U.S., from southern Canada south through the northern U.S. and along the Appalachians. Winters from southern Canada south throughout U.S.

Ruby-crowned kinglet

Regulus calendula

Aᴌᴛʜᴏᴜɢʜ ɪᴛ cannot be described as a regular feeder visitor, the ruby-crowned kinglet is more likely to show up there than its golden-crowned cousin. Suet is the preferred feeder food, although it will eat oil-type sunflower seeds. This is another species most likely to be seen among the mixed flocks of smaller birds during the winter. During this period woodland thickets and areas of thick undergrowth are the preferred habitat. Coniferous woodlands are generally selected for nesting areas. There the pair of birds builds a cuplike nest of grass, bits of bark and plant fibers. If available, lichen of the Usnea family also will be woven into the structure.

As the bird moves north to the breeding grounds in early spring, it tends to sing its chattering song. It is on the breeding grounds that the namesake crown of the male is most visible, usually puffed up in aggression for only a few seconds at a time.

Breeds from Alaska and northwestern Canada south throughout the western U.S. and east throughout central and southern Canada. Winters along Pacific Coast and from New York south in the east.

The ruby-crowned kinglet lays five to 11 off-white eggs spotted with red-brown in a fur- and feather-lined cup woven from twigs, plant fibers, moss and lichen. The nest is usually attached to twigs under a horizontal branch of a conifer anywhere from just above the ground to nearly 100 feet (30m) above.

Plumage
Brown-green above, lighter below; narrow white eyerings; red tufted crown. Female lacks red crown.

Bill
Short, thin, pointed, black.

Feet
Anisodactyl, dark reddish brown.

Body length
About 4 inches (10cm).

Size

Habitat
Coniferous woodlands; deciduous woodlands and thickets in winter.

Food
Insects and spiders; some fruits and berries in winter. At the feeder, suet and sometimes oil-type sunflower seeds.

Song
Varied chattering, with a definite musical quality.

Northern mockingbird

Mimus polyglottos

THE NORTHERN mockingbird is a good news/bad news type of bird. The good news is that the bird can learn and imitate the songs and calls of an incredible number of other bird species, as well as many other sounds ranging from a squeaky wheel to a human whistle to a dog's bark. Some birds have been recorded as mastering more than three dozen different sounds. The bad news is that one of the primary times the bird chooses to display this talent is in the middle of the night and, according to some accounts, a prime location is right outside the bedroom window.

The mockingbird is highly territorial, toward both others of its own species and nearly any other species that happen by. Although they are not feeder birds (other than the occasional attack on suet), they do squabble with other birds that would make use of feeders within the territory they claim. Hedgerows of thorny, berry-producing plants such as barberry provide both the preferred nesting locations and a ready source of winter food for the species. A backyard that provides such a feature will often maintain a resident mockingbird for many years, one generation of bird after another. One such backyard in central Pennsylvania has had its mockingbird for more than 40 years.

Breeds from southern Canada south throughout the U.S. Winters throughout California and as far north as New York and the western Great Lakes.

The northern mockingbird lays three to five pale blue or green eggs heavily spotted and blotched with brown in a rootlet-lined cluster of leaves, weed stems, hair and moss on a loosely intertwined platform of thorny twigs.

Brown thrasher
Toxostoma rufum

THE BROWN thrasher is a relatively secretive bird, often uncooperative in offering up its song or the songs of other species that it mimics. However, when the male does let loose, it can display the largest repertoire of any North American bird. The numbers have been documented at more than 1,200 songs and estimated at more than twice that many. It has been suggested that the male's ability to produce this enormous range of song determines in large part the quality of the territory and mate it will be able to claim. It usually sings from a perch high in the treetops. When it comes time for nest-building, however, the bird drops to near ground level.

The bird's name arises from its feeding habit of foraging through the leaf litter, thrashing its head and bill from side to side to expose the ground and insects or spiders hidden there. Only during severe winters will the thrasher come to feeders, where it will take suet and oil-type sunflower seeds. Year-round a more effective means of attracting it is to plant berry-producing, hedgerow-type plants, such as elderberry, hackberry, holly or mulberry, and provide a ready source of water.

Breeds throughout southern Canada and U.S. east of the Great Plains. Winters as far north as the Carolinas.

The brown thrasher lays two to five pale blue-white eggs spotted with red-brown in a rootlet-lined cup of twigs, grass stems, bits of vine, strips of bark and leaves. This is placed on a loose foundation of thorny twigs. The nest is usually on the ground under a shrub or as high as 14 feet (4.3m) in a tree, shrub or vines.

Spotter's Checklist

Plumage
Red-brown head, back, wings and tail; greenish brown around eyes and cheeks; white chin, breast and underside with large black and brown spots.

Bill
Large, pointed, black, with slight downward curve.

Feet
Anisodactyl, reddish gray.

Body length
About 11½ inches (29cm).

Size

Habitat
Woodland edges, thickets, brushy agricultural areas.

Food
Insects, spiders, fruits, berries and seeds. Not much of a feeder bird, but sometimes comes for sunflower seeds and suet.

Song
Series of whistling phrases repeated at least twice.

Gray catbird

Dumetella carolinensis

Spotter's Checklist

Plumage
Slate gray with black cap, wing tips and tail; red-brown under tail.

Bill
Long, pointed, black, with slight downward curve.

Feet
Anisodactyl, reddish brown.

Body length
About 8¾ inches (22cm).

Size

Habitat
Brushy areas, thickets, residential areas.

Food
About half insects and spiders, and half fruits, berries and seeds. Not much of a feeder bird, but during severe periods will come to suet, peanut butter and bits of apple.

Song
Series of seemingly disconnected harsh and rasping phrases; none repeated.

Named for its catlike mewing, the gray catbird is a fairly accomplished mimic. But unlike their close relations, the mockingbirds, catbirds manage only a jumbled, rambling rendition of those sounds they attempt to duplicate. Although the species is completely at home in backyards that provide hedgerows, thickets and brush piles, the birds tend to keep themselves secreted in the thick undergrowth. Berries make up a large proportion of the gray catbird's diet and plantings of species such as bittersweet, blueberry, cherry, elderberry, greenbrier, holly, honeysuckle, mulberry and pokeberry near thick cover will certainly attract them.

Those that decide to forego the fall migration tend to remain year-round in such an environment. However they choose to place their nests in evergreen shrubs and trees. In producing her offspring, the female gray catbird employs a curious means of incubation to match the number of new birds to the available food. She begins incubating the eggs she has laid first before she lays her entire clutch. This hatches some of her young well before the others and these nestlings are better able to compete for the food she brings back. In lean years however, this means that the nestlings hatched later may not get enough food.

Breeds from southern Canada south through the Rockies and east. Winters as far north as the Carolinas.

The gray catbird lays three to five dark green-blue eggs in a deep, rootlet-lined cup of grass and weed stems on a bulky foundation of grass, weed stems, vines, twigs, leaves and litter. The nest is usually placed in shrubs, low trees or clumps of vines from 3 to 20 feet (1-6m) off the ground.

Northern oriole

Icterus galbula

T HE NORTHERN oriole was formerly known as the Baltimore oriole, a name that that was originally given to the bird in the seventeenth century in honor of the Lords Baltimore of the colony of Maryland. A variety of this species with a somewhat different appearance — orange cheeks and eyebrow, and white wing patch — was formerly known as the Bullock's oriole, but is now also considered part of the northern oriole species. The link was confirmed when trees planted across the Great Plains provided a link between the ranges of the two populations and they interbred freely.

Most of the birds in both populations spend the winter months south of the U.S.

border, but those that remain are readily attracted to fruit halves placed in trees. Oranges are preferred and will attract the birds year-round. During extremely tough weather periods seeds may be taken. The northern oriole in the east builds a unique hanging, pendant-type nest of grass and other plant fibers decorated with spider webs, plant down and similar light-colored materials, such as yarn and twine. The former Bullock's oriole builds a simple cup of grass and plant fibers in the crook of a tree.

Breeds throughout most of the U.S., except for Deep South, and southern Canada.

The northern oriole lays four to six gray-white eggs scrawled and blotched with brown and black in a hair-, grass-, wool- and cotton-lined pouch woven from plant fibers, hair, vines, strips of bark, string and similar litter. The nest is usually attached at its rim to a hanging branch from 5 to 60 feet (1.5-18.2m) off the ground.

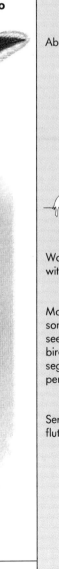

Spotter's Checklist

Plumage
Black head, back, wings and tail; orange breast, underside and bands on shoulders; white wing bars. Female greenish brown with duller underside and wing bars.

Bill
Long, pointed, silver.

Feet
Anisodactyl, silvery gray.

Body length
About 7¾ inches (20cm).

Size

Habitat
Woodlands, residential areas with mature shade trees.

Food
Mostly insects and spiders; some fruits, berries and seeds. Not much of a feeder bird, but will come for orange segments and, in severe periods, for seeds.

Song
Series of whistles with a flutelike quality.

Orchard oriole

Icterus spurius

Spotter's Checklist

Plumage
Black head, back, wings and tail; burnt orange breast, underside and bands on shoulders. Female yellowish buff with olive-brown wings; yellow below.

Bill
Long, pointed, black.

Feet
Anisodactyl, silvery gray.

Body length
About 7 inches (18cm).

Size

Habitat
Orchards, residential areas and waterways with shade trees.

Food
Mostly insects and spiders; some berries and seeds. Not a feeder bird.

Song
"Cheer-e-ly, cheer-ip, cheer-e-ly;" also a series of widely varied notes ending in "where."

The orchard oriole lays three to seven pale blue-white eggs, spotted and blotched with brown, purple and gray, in a grass-woven basket lined with plant down. The nest is usually hung between the forked branches of a tree or shrub from 5 to 70 feet (1.5-21.3m) off the ground.

IN SOME parts of its range, particularly the Deep South, the orchard oriole nests in dense clusters of other birds of its own kind. More than 20 hanging, pouch-like nests have been recorded in a single tree. Oaks are the preferred trees for such clusters, while fruit trees and other deciduous varieties are generally selected elsewhere with one nest to a tree being the norm. Trees along lakes and streams are often chosen.

The species is completely at home in manmade environments, ranging from backyards to orchards, and readily accepts nesting hand-outs such as plant fibers and bits of yarn from hanging baskets. If a pair intends to nest in or near a backyard, the male will be observed singing there daily. Offering such materials and planting fruit trees are about the only measures that can be taken to try to attract the species into a given backyard.

The orchard oriole is definitely not a feeder bird, as the entire population migrates south of the U.S. border for the winter. Breeds throughout U.S. east of the Great Plains.

Scott's oriole
Icterus parisorum

THE SCOTT'S oriole is one of the few North American species, other than hummingbirds, that will readily and regularly come to suspended bottles of sugar water. Also like hummingbirds, Scott's oriole will visit nectar-rich flowers. Unlike the hummingbirds, however, the oriole needs a perch to take advantage of the sugar water or the nectar, since it cannot hover while drinking.

A second measure to attract the species is to plant palm or yucca in the backyard to produce the sites where the birds prefer to construct their hanging, pendantlike nests. Fruit halves, particularly oranges, also can be placed in the crooks of trees. In addition to nectar and fruit, the Scott's oriole consumes many insects, which it gleans from a variety of trees, but particularly palm and yucca. As with all species of this dry region, water is a crucial element of its habitat. The Scott's oriole prefers moving or dripping water to standing water.

Breeds throughout the southwestern U.S. Winters to the south of the U.S.-Mexican border.

The Scott's oriole lays three to five blue-white eggs spotted with brown in a hanging pouch of grass.

Spotter's Checklist

Plumage
Black head, breast, back, wings and tail; bright yellow shoulder, lower breast, underside, flanks and rump. Female much duller.

Bill
Long, pointed, silver-gray.

Feet
Anisodactyl, silvery gray.

Body length
About 7 inches (18cm).

Size

Habitat
Dry yucca and pinyon areas.

Food
Insects, spiders, fruits, nectar from flowers. At the feeder, sugar-water bottles.

Song
Succession of chatters, whistles and warbles.

Common grackle
Quiscalus quiscula

THE COMMON grackle is one of the most aggressive birds in the backyard, generally arriving in flocks that actively dominate all other birds at the feeder. It also has been known to attack and kill smaller birds, mammals and reptiles. Their diet is incredibly catholic and includes almost any other edible being or morsel that the birds encounter. However the big, black birds prefer to feed at ground level and will accept nearly any type of seed or table scrap offered there, a characteristic that can be employed to keep them away from the elevated feeders maintained for less aggressive species.

Although the common grackle occurs across nearly all habitat types within its range, it is particularly common around human dwellings and other areas where litter can be found for scavenging. Grackles are among the various black birds that gather into huge flocks to migrate south each fall. Such flocks can cause a great deal of localized agricultural damage, and at times have come under attack from farmers. Although the common grackle's eyes are generally described as bright yellow, in fact they start out brown in younger birds and become paler with age.

Breeds from central Canada south, east of the Rockies. Winters as far north as the Great Lakes and Connecticut, but not in Appalachians.

The common grackle lays three to six pale green-brown eggs spotted and blotched with purple and dark brown in a grass-, feather- and debris-lined bowl woven from weed stems, grass and debris. The nest is usually one in a colony of 20 to 30 placed anywhere from 1 to 60 feet (0.3-18.2m) off the ground in trees, shrubs or cavities.

Boat-tailed grackle
Quiscalus major

Boat-tailed grackles nest in colonies, filling trees with their large, untidy nests. The adult birds maintain a near-constant chatter of various squeaks and electronic-like sounds that can be almost deafening in larger colonies. This noise is also common when roaming, foraging flocks settle into trees in our parks and backyards. This is a characteristic shared with the closely related common grackle, which is generally smaller and lacks the V-shaped tail.

Flocks range across relatively large territories, and the fact that they nest in a given backyard does not mean they will frequent feeders there. On the other hand, they just might. They do come readily to feeders, preferring to feed at ground level. Cracked corn, sunflower seeds and bread crumbs are among their favorite foods. Like the common grackle, the boat-tailed species joins the mixed flocks of black birds that migrate in thousands each fall.

Resident along Atlantic Coast from New York south and along Gulf of Mexico.

Spotter's Checklist

Plumage
Black with iridescent green-and-blue tint; keel-shaped tail. Female brown with pale breast.

Bill
Long, stout, pointed, slate gray.

Feet
Anisodactyl, slate gray.

Body length
About 16½ inches (42cm).

Size

Habitat
Wetlands; agricultural areas near wetlands.

Food
Very catholic diet. At the feeder, nearly everything that's offered.

Song
"Jeep-jeep-jeep-jeep," rasping.

The boat-tailed grackle lays two to five pale blue-gray eggs, spotted and scrawled with brown, gray, black and purple, in a mud- and grass-lined cup. This is loosely made from grass and weed stems and placed on a foundation of vines, rushes and grass. The nest is usually one in a colony built in bulrushes, cattails or willows from 1 to 4 feet (0.3-1.2m) off the ground, or in trees as much as 50 feet (15.2m) off the ground.

Red-winged blackbird

Agelaius phoeniceus

Spotter's Checklist

Plumage
Black with orange and yellow shoulder epaulet. Female and young streaked buff and gray-brown.

Bill
Long, stout, pointed, slate gray.

Feet
Anisodactyl, black.

Body length
About 8¼ inches (21 cm).

Size

Habitat
Meadows, wetlands.

Food
Insects, spiders and seeds. At the feeder, cracked corn and sunflower seeds.

Song
"Con-car-eeeeeee;" also "tse-rr, tse-rr;" also "chuck."

THE RED-winged blackbird is primarily a bird of the marshes and wet meadows, but individual birds, pairs and flocks can be spotted along nearly any waterway and often in dry pastureland. Insects form the bulk of the bird's diet in summer, but it is quick to take advantage of nearby feeders, particularly during migration and the winter months. Nearly any type of seed is taken, although cracked corn and sunflower seeds top the list. They are not a highly predictable feeder bird, outside of the fact that at some time every feeder within their territory will be visited. When they do appear , often it will be with an explosion of noise and movement. Generally they will stay for a long time and consume a great deal of seed.

Although sizeable portions of the population do not migrate, the red-winged blackbird is another of the many different blackbird species that gather into huge flocks in the fall for a southward movement. As these flocks mass in the south during the winter, some have been estimated at more than 10 million birds. In such masses the birds, which may be beneficial insect controls in smaller numbers back on their northern breeding grounds, can become major agricultural pests.

Breeds throughout the U.S. and southern Canada north through western Canada into Alaska. Winters across the southern half of the U.S., further north along both coasts.

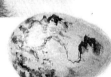

The red-winged blackbird lays three or four pale blue-green eggs, spotted, blotched and scrawled with black, purple and brown, in a grass-lined cup of weed stems. Placed on a platform of rushes, grass, sedges and rootlets, it is securely bound to support plants with milk-weed fibers. The nest is usually part of a loose colony and is placed anywhere from a few inches to 15 feet (4.6m) off the ground.

Brewer's blackbird

Euphagus cyanocephalus

Brewer's blackbird, named for Dr. Thomas Brewer, the nineteenth-century ornithologist from Boston, is a very gregarious species most often seen in sizeable flocks. These flocks forage across all sorts of grassy and weedy areas in search of the insects and spiders that make up most of their diet. After agricultural fields have been harvested the flocks switch over to these, gleaning whatever grain has fallen from the harvesting machines. Often the birds nest in equally sizeable colonies, using the nesting area as their base from which they go off on their foraging flights. They turn to feeders primarily in the winter, although properties near agricultural areas may be visited at other times.

Ground-level feeding is preferred with any type of seed being taken. The birds tend to breed and nest in hayfields or in low trees, and might be encouraged to set up housekeeping in a field-type backyard. The effort is worthwhile to observe the breeding season display, when the birds fluff out their feathers, quiver their wings, flick and cock their tails and arch their necks.

Breeds from southcentral and southwestern Canada south throughout the western half of the U.S. Winters across southeastern, southcentral and western U.S.

The Brewer's blackbird lays three to seven green-gray eggs, spotted and blotched with gray and brown, in a rootlet-, grass-, and hair-lined bowl made of sturdily interwoven twigs and grass reinforced with mud or manure. The nest is usually placed either on the ground in heavy weeds, or in shrubs or trees as much as 150 feet (46m) off the ground, sometimes as part of a loose colony.

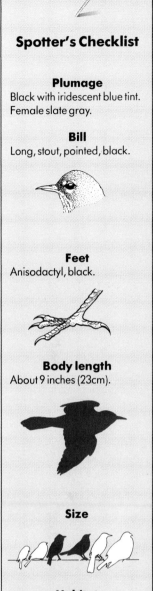

Spotter's Checklist

Plumage
Black with iridescent blue tint. Female slate gray.

Bill
Long, stout, pointed, black.

Feet
Anisodactyl, black.

Body length
About 9 inches (23cm).

Size

Habitat
Agricultural areas, prairies.

Food
Seeds, fruits, insects and spiders. At the feeder, very catholic appetite.

Song
Various whistles and squawks.

European starling
Sturnus vulgaris

The European starling lays four to seven blue- or green-white eggs. The nest is a mass of grass, weed stems, twigs, leaves, feathers, cloth and other debris in a cavity anywhere from 2 to 60 feet (0.6-18.2m) off the ground. At the center of the nest mass is a cup of fine grass and feathers.

NEARLY EVERYTHING negative that can be said about species introduced to new habitat by humans has been said about the starling, usually with a great deal of truth. The species competes aggressively and successfully with native species for nesting cavities and food. Flocks can do a great deal of damage in both the backyard garden and the farmer's fields. They tend to congregate around human habitations, making a mess. On the other hand, starlings eat an incredible number of harmful insects.

Whichever side of the debate you come down on, you have to admit that the species is enormously adaptable. Since the first 100 birds were released in Central Park in New York City in 1890-91 by a Shakespeare fan who wanted to give America all the birds mentioned in the works of the great writer, the species has spread out and occupied the whole of the United States, the southern half of Canada (all the way to southern Alaska along the Pacific Coast) and northern Mexico. Absolutely nothing needs to be done to attract the birds into the backyard for feeding or nesting. If there's any food there whatsoever they will come to feed. If there are any potential cavities, from rain spouts to tree hollows, they will come to nest.

Resident from central Canada south throughout U.S., further north along both coasts.

Brown-headed cowbird
Molothrus ater

THE BROWN-headed cowbird and the closely related bronzed cowbird are unique among all songbirds of North America in their habits of nesting and rearing their young. In short, they do neither. Instead, the female lays her eggs in the nests of other birds and thus ends her family obligations. The eggs are left for the host birds — more than 200 species have been counted — to brood and hatch. Some of the parasitized species push the intruding egg from their nest. Others simply build a new nest bottom over the cowbird's eggs, leaving the latter to rot. Most, however, go about their normal hatching duties and then parent the cowbird chick with their own. The foreign chick tends to grow faster than the chicks of most host parents, capturing most of the food brought back to the nest by the parents and often crowding the true offspring right out of the nest.

The number of species parasitized by the cowbirds has increased dramatically since European settlers arrived in North America. Previously the birds were confined primarily to the plains and prairies region, where they followed the bison herds and foraged on the insects the big animals stirred up. But, as the European settlers opened similarly large expanses, the cowbirds found new territories through which they could forage and quickly moved into them, finding an entirely new group of birds to serve as unwitting foster parents for their chicks.

Breeds throughout southern Canada and U.S., except for Florida. Winters as far north as Maryland and southern California.

Spotter's Checklist

Plumage
Black with brown head. Female gray-brown.

Bill
Short, pointed, gray.

Feet
Anisodactyl, black.

Body length
About 7 inches (18cm).

Size

Habitat
Aricultural areas, residential areas, woodland edges.

Food
Seeds, berries and fruits; some insects and spiders. At the feeder, cracked corn, sunflower seeds and bread crumbs.

Song
"Double, double, zeee."

The brown-headed cowbird lays its gray-white eggs spotted with brown in the nests of other birds, for the other birds to hatch and rear. The female usually lays one egg per day until her entire clutch of six or more has been deposited in nests.

Eastern meadowlark
Sturnella magna

Spotter's Checklist

Plumage
Streaked brown and white above, white-edged tail, bright yellow throat and breast, black "V" across breast.

Bill
Long, stout, conical, black over gray-blue.

Feet
Anisodactyl, pale gray-blue.

Body length
About 10 inches (25cm).

Size

Habitat
Agricultural areas, meadows, prairies; residential areas in migration.

Food
Insects, spiders and seeds. Not a feeder bird.

Song
"Bring-all-your-gear, bring-all-your-gear," usually followed by a rattle.

FIELDS AND grasslands are the natural haunts of the eastern meadowlark, which is not a lark at all but a member of the blackbird family. The bird's long legs, long bill, grass-camouflaged back, and predator-startling bright breast and outer tail feathers are all adaptations to this grassy existence. Grainfields are a favored habitat type, but more for the insects that they attract than the grain itself. The meadowlark generally takes the grain only during severe winter periods. It also shows a penchant for moving into orchards at such times to supplement its diet with missed fruit, particularly apples. Feeders and bird baths will not attract the bird, but properties located near fields and grasslands within the species' range will more than likely have some of the birds nearby. They will not be difficult to see or hear.

A distinct western species, *Sturnella neglecta,* shares both appearance and habit with the eastern meadowlark, although the song is entirely different. The two populations have been found to be separate species because where their ranges overlap they do not interbreed.

Breeds across the eastern half of the U.S. and southern Canada. Winters as far north as Connecticut and Illinois.

The eastern meadowlark lays two to six white eggs, spotted and blotched with brown and purple (more heavily at the large end), in a small depression on the ground. Lined first with grass and then with finer grasses and hair, the nest also has a dome-shaped grass canopy over the top.

Cedar waxwing
Bombycilla cedrorum

SMALL FRUITS and berries make up the bulk of the cedar waxwing's diet during the spring, fall and winter. However, during the summer, the birds switch largely to insects, taking them in flight like the various flycatcher species. Large flocks are often seen attacking whatever hatch of insects is now rising into the air. As each bird grabs an insect it returns to its perch to eat.

The young are fed a relatively large proportion of fruits and berries that are stored in the adult's crop and regurgitated into their waiting mouths. For this reason cedar waxwings normally nest late in the season, when the fruits and berries are most plentiful. The birds generally travel in flocks, when individual pairs are not nesting, and are quite social. Lines of the birds perched along a branch are often seen passing a berry or fruit blossom from one to the next. Eventually one of the birds along the way will gobble the offering and the process will start anew.

The cedar waxwing is not a feeder bird, but flocks come readily to backyards planted with fruit trees and berry bushes. Fruits and berries left on the plants into the winter will attract them, as will fresh water.

Breeds throughout southern Canada and northern U.S. Winters throughout southern U.S., as far north as New York and the Great Lakes and all along the Pacific Coast.

The cedar waxwing lays two to six pale blue-gray eggs spotted with brown and brown-gray. The nest is a rootlet-, grass- and plant down-lined bowl loosely woven from twigs, grass, weed stems, string and downy fibers. It is usually placed on a horizontal branch from 4 to 50 feet (1.2-15.2m) off the ground.

Spotter's Checklist

Plumage
Greenish-brown with black mask, red waxy-looking tips on wing feathers and yellow tips on tail feathers.

Bill
Short, rounded, black, slight downward curve.

Feet
Anisodactyl, black.

Body length
About 7¼ inches (18cm).

Size

Habitat
Orchards, woodlands; residential areas, particularly those with fruit and berry plants.

Food
Mostly berries and seeds, but some insects. Not a feeder bird.

Song
"Zeee, zeee, zeee, zeee."

Common yellowthroat
Geothlypis trichas

WHEN IT comes to courtship, the male common yellowthroat is one of the most exuberant birds of North America. At any point in the breeding season, the little guy may suddenly flutter up into the air, bursting out with a jumbled mix of excited song (known as ecstasy song), and then falling back into the grass. He's also likely to belt out the normal "witchity-witchity-witchity-witchity-wit" song at any time of the day or night. The species is similarly enthusiastic about defending its territory. Nearly any perceived intruder is likely to be scolded by the bird, which suddenly pops out of some thicket or tangle. A squeaking noise will excite the scolding to even greater heights.

The common yellowthroat prefers a secretive existence in the tangled understory and thickets, particularly along waterways and swamps. Its diet is almost entirely insects, spiders and worms. The species is not a feeder bird, although it might be attracted into a backyard that offers the type of habitat described above.

Breeds from central Canada south throughout the U.S. Winters as far north as the southern U.S.

The common yellowthroat lays three to six off-white eggs spotted with brown, gray and black. The nest is a grass-, bark strip- and hair-lined basket loosely woven of grass, reed shreds and leaves, securely attached to surrounding weed stalks or low brush.

Yellow warbler
Dendroica petechia

Spotter's Checklist

Plumage
Brown back and wings with dull yellow bars; yellow-orange head, chin, breast and underside with red-brown streaks. Female lacks red-brown streaks.

Bill
Long, stout, rounded, black.

Feet
Anisodactyl, silvery gray.

Body length
About 4¾ inches (12cm).

Size

Habitat
Residential areas, brushy areas along waterways, wetlands.

Food
Mostly insects and spiders; some fruits and berries. Not a regular feeder visitor.

Song
"Sweet, sweet, sweet, bitter-nor-sweet."

THE YELLOW warbler is one of the most widespread warblers of North America. It also is one of the warblers most likely to appear in the backyard. However, it is not a feeder bird but almost entirely an insect-eater that migrates south of the United States for the winter.

Moist habitats clogged with thickets and heavy undergrowth are the primary attraction for the birds. They are most active during the spring breeding season, when males can be found frantically flitting about their territories chasing off every trespasser or singing loudly from the top branches of some shrub. They continue their song while they gather materials such as bits of bark and plant down for nests.

These small, but sturdy cup-shaped nests are one of the primary targets of the parasitic cowbird. In response the yellow warbler adds a new bottom to the nest, right over the cowbird egg and often over some of its own, and begins to lay a new clutch. This may happen several times during the nesting season. Yellow warbler nests have been found with a half-dozen new bottoms, each covering an offending cowbird egg.

Breeds continentwide except for northernmost Canada and Deep South U.S.

The yellow warbler lays three to five blue- or gray-white eggs splotched with brown and gray. The nest is a plant down-, hair- and grass-lined cup securely woven from grass, milkweed plant fibers and plant down. It is usually placed in the fork of a tree or shrub from 2 to 12 feet (0.6-3.6m) off the ground.

Yellow-rumped warbler
Dendroica coronata

Spotter's Checklist

Plumage
Blue-gray streaked with black above; two white wing bars; breast and underside dark gray; yellow rump and crown. Female and male in fall/winter streaked gray and brown with yellow rump.

Bill
Short, stout, rounded, black.

Feet
Anisodactyl, dark gray.

Body length
About 5½ inches (14cm).

Size

Habitat
Woodlands; residential areas in winter.

Food
Insects, spiders, fruits, berries and seeds. Not a feeder bird.

Song
"Check;" also a buzzing warble.

IN THE east the yellow-rumped warbler is the only warbler that can be expected to spend the winter months in the northern states. Here it was formerly known as the myrtle warbler, which was thought to be a distinct species from the western Audubon's warbler. However, where the ranges of the two intersect they interbreed freely and thus are really one species. The two populations can be differentiated largely by their mostly distinct ranges, although they also show some variations in coloration.

The yellow-rumped warbler is primarily an insect-eater. In some locations it has been dubbed the "spider bird" for its ability to dart among buildings and other structures, plucking spiders from their webs and from the sides of the buildings. However the significant numbers of the bird that remain in the north through the winter supplement their diets heavily with berries. Preferred berry plants are bayberry, juniper and sumac. Plantings of these interspersed with mature trees are the most promising measures to attract the species.

Breeds from Alaska and northwestern Canada south and east to Mexico and New York. A substantial proportion of the population winters along the U.S. Pacific Coast and southern U.S.

The yellow-rumped warbler lays three to five white eggs spotted and blotched with brown, often more heavily at the large end, in a feather-, hair- and grass-lined cup woven loosely of twigs, strips of bark and plant fibers. The nest is usually placed on a horizontal branch of a conifer, generally near the trunk, from 5 to 50 feet (1.5-15.2m) off the ground.

Yellow-throated warbler

Dendroica dominica

THE YELLOW- throated warbler is extremely trusting and regularly feeds almost within grasping range. It comes readily into the backyard in pursuit of insects and spiders, which make up almost all of its diet. Fruit that attracts insects may in turn attract the bird, which may then add a bit of the fruit to its meal. Seeds are taken only during periods of extreme deprivation. The yellow-throated warbler prefers to place its small cuplike nest of plant fibers, down, spider webs and bits of bark in clumps of Spanish moss and is attracted to locations that include this plant even outside of the nesting season. The bird is generally active, foraging for insects and spiders among the treetops, but it will drop to the forest floor when the feeding appears more promising there.

Breeds from New Jersey and Illinois south throughout the U.S.; winters in the Gulf states.

The yellow-throated warbler lays three to five green- or gray-white eggs spotted with brown and gray. The nest is a grass-, feather- and moss-lined, cup-shaped pocket placed either in a tangle of Spanish moss (in coastal areas), or in the fork of a tree (inland) between 10 and 100 feet (3-30m) off the ground.

Spotter's Checklist

Plumage
Grayish back, shoulders and wings, with bands of white and black on wings; black eye and cheek areas; spotted black along sides; yellow throat; off-white underside.

Bill
Long, rounded, black.

Feet
Anisodactyl, brown-gray.

Body length
About 5 inches (13cm).

Size

Habitat
Woodlands.

Food
Mostly insects and spiders; some fruits in winter. Comes to feeders only during severe periods.

Song
"Teeu-teeu-teeu-teeu-two-two-twee."

Black-and-white warbler
Mniotilta varia

Spotter's Checklist

Plumage
Striped black and white, broad at cap and on sides, finer at neck, breast and shoulders, black throat. Female has white throat.

Bill
Large, rounded, black.

Feet
Anisodactyl, black.

Body length
About 5 inches (13cm).

Size

Habitat
Deciduous woodlands; residential areas in migration.

Food
Insects and spiders. Sometimes comes to suet.

Song
"Wee-saw, wee-saw, wee-saw, wee-saw."

THIS SPECIES was once known as the black-and-white creeper for its habit of foraging for insects by creeping about on tree trunks and branches. But its current designation as the black-and-white warbler is more accurate. This small, striped bird does move up the tree trunk like the brown creeper, but it also can travel headfirst down the trunk, a nuthatch-type feat that creepers cannot manage. The black-and-white warbler is often observed feeding in mixed flocks with other warbler and chickadee species.

A relatively small proportion of the population winters in the Deep South, but most birds travel to northern South America. The species returns to its northern breeding grounds early each spring, generally no later than mid-April and well before most other species. The zebra-striping of the bird makes it one of the easiest of all warbler species to identify when it turns up near human habitations, which happens most frequently during migration.

Breeds from southern Canada south through the U.S. east of the Rockies. Winters as far north as the Gulf states.

The black-and-white warbler lays three to five off-white eggs lightly spotted with brown in a grass-lined cup at the center of a mound of dry leaves, grass, strips of vine, rootlets and weed stems. The nest is usually placed on the ground at the base of a tree, log, stump or rock.

White-eyed vireo
Vireo griseus

U NLIKE MOST other species of vireo, the white-eyed vireo generally is found in forest thickets rather than among the treetops. The first indication of its presence is most often its easily recognized song, although the species is relatively curious and generally will approach an observer who remains very still for a closer inspection. The species is readily identified by its bright yellow mask, although its namesake feature — the white eyes — usually can be discerned only at relatively close quarters.

Decidedly an insect-eater, the white-eyed vireo will take some berries during periods of extreme deprivation. As such the species is not a regular feeder visitor, but it can be attracted into backyards with dense thickets. Berry-producing shrubs and vines produce the thickets that are most attractive to the white-eyed vireo for their double-punch of shelter and food. Greenbriar and honeysuckle have been suggested as the bird's preferences.

Breeds from Great Lakes and New York south throughout the eastern U.S.; winters as far north as the Gulf Coast.

The white-eyed vireo lays three to five white eggs sparsely spotted with brown or black. The nest is a plant stem- and grass-lined cone woven securely from strips of bark, pieces of soft wood, and insect and spider silk. It is suspended from a fork in a shrub or tree between 1 and 8 feet (0.3-2.4m) off the ground.

Spotter's Checklist

Plumage
Brownish green on back and sides, yellowish at eyes and flanks, white wing bars, buff underside.

Bill
Long, rounded, black.

Feet
Anisodactyl, blue-gray.

Body length
About 5 inches (13cm).

Size

Habitat
Thickets, particularly berry-producers; wetlands.

Food
Insects and spiders; some berries. Not a feeder bird.

Song
"Chick-per-a-wee-o-chick."

Red-eyed vireo
Vireo olivaceus

THE RED-eyed vireo, once a common resident of eastern and northern woodlands, has suffered significant population losses in recent years through the destruction of its habitat. The forests of the species' northern breeding grounds have been cut into fragmented sections, a condition that is injurious to a species that needs large expanses of uninterrupted woodlands. The opening of corridors into the wooded areas also has opened the species to the previously unencountered nest-parasitism by cowbirds. This phenomenon has cut drastically into the populations of many woodland songbirds. But for birds that winter in the tropics and thus have time to bring off only one clutch of eggs each summer, the impact is even more serious. And the Amazonian rainforest, where the red-eyed vireo winters, is being destroyed at an alarming rate.

Tall trees, particularly deciduous woodlands, surrounded by thick undergrowth are the favored home of the species. Because it only rarely eats anything other than insects, the red-eyed vireo can be attracted into the backyard only through proper habitat.

Breeds from central Canada south through the U.S. into Texas and Florida.

The red-eyed vireo lays two to four white eggs sparsely spotted with brown and black. The nest is a deep cup tightly woven from grass, strips of bark, paper, rootlets and small vines covered on the outside with lichen. It is attached to the twigs of a fork in a tree branch anywhere from 2 to 50 feet (0.6-15.2m) off the ground.

American redstart
Setophaga ruticilla

THE AMERICAN redstart is one of the most abundant birds throughout its range, which has expanded as humanity's development of the continent has left more and more of the bird's favorite habitat type: second-growth woodland. Such dense undergrowth is a critical habitat factor, which can be developed to attract the species. Such a property should be expected to attract at least a few of the birds each year, since particularly during the fall migration a staggering number of the birds moves south. Water, too, is a powerful attraction for the redstart. It is not a feeder bird; its diet is nearly all insects supplemented with some fruits and berries.

The male redstart is slow to develop its beautiful orange and black plumage, a process that often requires a full two years. This leads to the mistaken impression that the female also is a songster, when in fact it is the immature males that are singing. The American redstart seems to be constantly in motion as it hops along a branch, or hovers or falls through the air fluttering its wings, and snatching at insects.

Breeds from Alaska and central Canada south to Louisiana in the east and throughout the Rockies. Winters south of the U.S.-Mexican border.

The American redstart lays two to five off-white eggs spotted and blotched with brown and gray, often more heavily at the large end. The nest is a grass-, weed stem-, hair- and feather-lined cup, tightly woven from bark strips, plant down, rootlets and grass, held together with insect and spider silk and decorated on the outside with lichen. It is placed in the fork of a tree or shrub from 4 to 25 feet (1.2-7.6m) off the ground.

Blue jay
Cyanocitta cristata

THE BLUE jay is a big, raucous bird that is never shy about making its location known. Anyone who has ever tried to sneak silently through a woodland inhabited by blue jays has had occasion to curse their alerted cry. Nothing escapes their notice and nothing that they notice goes unreported to the rest of the world. They bring this habit with them into the backyard, where they quickly become regular visitors to any feeder that is stocked with sunflower seeds, peanuts or other nuts. They generally travel in small bands of two to four during the winter, and their daily appearance — sometimes twice daily — will occur on an almost clocklike schedule. Every visit will be announced with their loud, piercing "jay-jay." They are domineering bullies at the feeder, although they generally stay on hand for only short periods at a time. They can be easily diverted from feeders used by other birds by separate placements of nuts. All sorts of nuts — particularly when offered in small piles on a feeding platform — will readily attract the jays' attention.

Resident throughout the U.S. and southern Canada east of the Rockies.

The blue jay lays three to six green-brown or tan eggs spotted with dark brown and gray in a rootlet-lined bulky bowl loosely woven from thorny twigs, strips of bark, string and leaves. The nest is usually placed in the fork of a tree branch from 5 to 50 feet (1.5-15.2m) off the ground.

Gray jay
Perisoreus canadensis

MANY NICKNAMES have been applied to the gray jay and most seem to have one word in common: "Robber." Anything that the active gray bird can carry is considered fair game. Lunch spread out upon the picnic table, fresh-caught fish, backpacker's stash hung aloft to escape bear pilfering, backwoods caches are all easy pickings to the gray jay. The report of gunfire has been known to bring the bird in a hurry to see what creature may now be available for feasting, and it's not uncommon for a gray jay to snatch food right out of the frying pan or from a human diner's hand. The species is entirely without shyness toward humanity. Is it any wonder then that anyone with a backyard feeder within the bird's range will be familiar with at least a few of this species? Large items, such as nuts, table scraps and sunflower seeds, are eagerly carted off by the birds, which cache most of the items in trees and shrubs nearby.

Even in the middle of winter the gray jay continues its caching against possible future periods of deprivation. This habit generally maintains the bird well througout the winter and, as a result, the species is a very early nester. Some have been observed on the nest as early as late February.

Resident throughout Alaska, central and southern Canada, U.S. Pacific Northwest and throughout the Rockies.

The gray jay lays two to five pale gray or green eggs spotted with darker green. The nest is a grass-, feather- and hair-lined cup woven tightly from twigs, grass, insect and spider silk, and strips of bark. It is usually placed on a conifer branch near the trunk from 4 to 25 feet (1.2-7.6m) off the ground.

Spotter's Checklist

Plumage
Gray above, darker at cap, eyeline and nape of neck; gray-white cheeks, breast and underside.

Bill
Long, stout, pointed, black.

Feet
Anisodactyl, dark gray.

Body length
About 12 inches (30cm).

Size

Habitat
Coniferous woodlands.

Food
Very catholic diet. At the feeder, seeds, cracked corn, suet, bread crumbs.

Song
"Wee-ah, chuck-chuck;" also a wide variety of screams.

Steller's jay
Cyanocitta stelleri

Plumage
Crested black head, fading to gray across breast and shoulders, slate gray tail, bright blue across rest of body.

Bill
Long, stout, pointed, silvery.

Feet
Anisodactyl, silvery.

Body length
About 11 inches (28cm).

Size

Habitat
Wooded areas, with at least some conifers.

Food
Fruit, seeds, nuts, insects. At the feeder, nuts, oil-type sunflower seeds, cracked corn.

Song
"Jay, jay, jay;" also "ca-weedle, ca-weedle, ca-weedle."

The Steller's jay lays three to five green eggs spotted with darker green in a rootlet- and plant fiber-lined bowl of twigs. The nest is usually placed in a conifer from 5 to 20 feet (1.5-6m) off the ground.

WHAT THE blue jay is to the eastern half of the U.S. and southern Canada, the Stellar's jay is to the West. It's a raucous, roaming bird that spends its day moving from one regular source of food to the next, announcing its arrival at each new location. It then carries off an ample supply of whatever nuts or large seeds — pine nuts and acorns are preferred — one by one. Most of these are cached in nearby nooks and crannies. The Steller's jay also is not above raiding the caches of other bird species, notably those of the acorn woodpeckers.

Although backyards throughout the range of the Steller's jay will be visited on an almost daily schedule throughout the year, so long as food is available on each visit, the winter generally will see an increase in the number of birds. At this time of the year additional family groups that have spent the rest of the year in the mountains move their foraging activities to the more amply stocked lowlands.

The Steller's jay shares many of the negative aspects of its eastern cousin, including a bullying attitude at the feeder and a taste for the eggs and nestlings of other birds. Also like the blue jay, this western species can mimic the attack scream of a red-tailed hawk.

Resident from southeastern Alaska and west-central Canada south throughout the western half of the U.S.

American crow

Corvus brachyrhynchos

AGRICULTURAL AREAS attract the largest flocks of American crows. But even center city environs have attracted the opportunistic attentions of the species, which has found nearly every type of manmade habitat to its liking. The crow is one of the most adaptable and intelligent birds on Earth. Although the small flocks of two or three birds that generally roam suburban neighborhoods may seem to be at ease in close proximity to humans, they really do not permit all that close an approach, and one of their number is always on guard.

The crow possesses one of the most catholic diets of all bird species. Just about anything organic can serve as the feast of the moment. Its reputation as a thief of the eggs and nestlings of other birds is well known, but its abilities as a predator are much less widely recognized. Any creature smaller than itself is open to attack. Even larger birds, such as owls and hawks, are not safe. The crows attack these birds as a flock and with great ferocity, not in pursuit of a kill but simply because the raptors represent a threat and must be driven from the territory.

Breeds from central Canada south throughout the U.S. Winters throughout U.S.

The American crow lays three to eight blue- or gray-green eggs spotted and blotched with darker gray and brown. The nest is a basket woven from sticks, twigs, strips of bark and vines and lined with bark strips, moss, grass, feathers and fur. The nest is usually in the fork of a tree or on a heavy limb from 20 to 75 feet (6-23m) off the ground.

Spotter's Checklist

Plumage
Black, fan-shaped tail.

Bill
Very large, broad and stout; black.

Feet
Anisodactyl, black.

Body length
About 20 inches (51 cm).

Size

Habitat
Woodland, agricultural and residential areas.

Food
Completely catholic diet. At the feeder, corn on cob, table scraps, suet.

Song
"Caw, caw, caw;" also a wide variety of rattles and clicks.

Black-billed magpie
Pica pica

Crows, Jays and Magpies: Corvidae

Spotter's Checklist

Plumage
Black with large, stark white shoulder patches, flanks and underside; tail as long as body.

Bill
Large, broad, stout, dark gray.

Feet
Anisodactyl, black.

Body length
About 20 inches (51 cm).

Size

Habitat
Coniferous woodlands, thickets along waterways.

Food
Very catholic diet. At the feeder, almost anything edible.

Song
"Wink, wink," with an almost echoing quality at the end of each note; also a variety of chattering and scolding.

The black-billed magpie lays six to nine brown-green eggs blotched with darker brown in a domed cup of often thorny twigs. The nest has two entrances and is usually placed in a small tree or shrub less than 30 feet (9m) off the ground.

THE BLACK-billed magpie is widely despised by those westerners who share its territory on a day-to-day basis, but marveled at by eastern visitors with no similar native species in their own backyards. Westerners have come to see the bird as a thief, a scavenger and a predator. Like the crows to which it's related, the black-billed magpie is adaptable enough to make a meal out of just about anything organic. Also like the crows, the magpie is an opportunistic predator, ready and able to kill and eat nearly anything smaller than its rather large self. However, the magpie has shown a much greater tendency to prey on domesticated animals. Young poultry are an easy target, as are large livestock with injuries.

Visiting easterners, in contrast, notably in national parks such as Yellowstone, see only a magnificently large bird with a flashy white and black plumage, a long flowing tail and the endearing quality of coming in for close observation when pilfering or scavenging food.

The species is easy to attract to nearly any type of food and feeder, so long as the feeder is not placed under trees or in an otherwise confining situation.

Resident from southern Alaska south along the Pacific Coast and east into central Canada, and south throughout the northern half of the western U.S.

Barn swallow
Hirundo rustica

THE BARN swallow is the most easily identified of our swallow species, with its sharply forked tail. The species is widespread and chances are that if swooping swallows are part of your memory you've encountered these birds. They are completely at home in close proximity to humans and take their common name from their penchant for nesting in and around our buildings, and in nearly any other structure with ready access, such as bridges and culverts.

The first indication that the birds are considering a site will be spotting them sitting on the topmost branch of a nearby tree or a power line. From that location, both birds make several inspection flights to the exact spot under consideration. The barn swallow generally nests in colonies near fields and waterways. The air in the vicinity of such a colony seems to be in constant motion and the birds keep up a regular twittering chorus. The amount of air miles flown every day by each of the birds has been estimated in the hundreds, as they search for and snatch up the flying insects that make up nearly all of their diet. They even drink and bathe while in flight, which explains why they are specially attracted to backyard sprinklers and agricultural irrigators.

Breeds from Alaska and central Canada south throughout the U.S. Winters in South America.

The barn swallow lays four to six white eggs spotted with brown in a bowl of mud pellets and straw lined with feathers (particularly white ones). The nest is plastered to beams and walls in farm buildings, under bridges and similar structures.

Spotter's Checklist

Plumage
Dark steel-blue above, buff below, red-brown forehead and throat; sharply forked tail.

Bill
Short, rounded, black.

Feet
Anisodactyl, black.

Body length
About 6¾ inches (17 cm).

Size

Habitat
Agricultural areas, residential areas, wetlands, waterways.

Food
Mostly insects; some berries. Not a feeder bird.

Song
Non-stop chatter and twittering.

Tree swallow

Tachycineta bicolor

Spotter's Checklist

Spotter's Checklist

Plumage
Dark metallic green-tinted blue above, white below. Young are dull brown above, white below.

Bill
Short, rounded, black.

Feet
Anisodactyl, black.

Body length
About 5¾ inches (14cm).

Size

Habitat
Open, grassy areas with dead trees, near water.

Food
Almost entirely insects; some berries in fall. Not a feeder bird.

Song
A rolling twitter.

ALTHOUGH THE tree swallow's diet for most of the year is made up almost exclusively of insects, the bird also is able to supplement that menu with berries, notably bayberries. This behavior allows the species to winter farther north than any of our other swallow species. Barn swallows annually spend their winters as far north as North Carolina in the east and southern California in the west. In milder years they have been sighted as far north as Cape Cod. However, all this does not mean that the tree swallow is not a migrant.

Each fall incredibly large flocks of the birds gather pre-migration along the coast, circling continuously like dust and leaves captured in the winds of a cyclone. Like all swallows, this species appears to take great pleasure in its considerable flying abilities. Individuals are often spotted toying with a floating feather, snatching it off a breeze and then dropping it only to catch it again and again.

There is nothing that will attract the tree swallow to a feeder, but the bird comes readily to use any nest box placed in an open location. Water, too, is a major attraction for tree swallows.

Breeds from Alaska and central Canada south through the northern half of the U.S. Has been known to winter as far north as southern Connecticut, although more commonly north only to South Carolina.

The tree swallow lays four to six white eggs in a cavity, in a mass of dry grass thickly lined with feathers.

Cliff swallow

Hirundo pyrrhonota

THE CLIFF swallow is the species that has given rise to the fame of San Juan Capistrano, where they return each year on a given day to their nesting sites at the Mission. They return equally faithfully to other nesting sites throughout their considerable breeding range each spring unless they've somehow been disturbed. But no other location has taken the return so to heart as Capistrano.

Back at their nesting sites the birds build circular nests from collections of small mud balls. They tend to live in colonies and often cover large walls with their nests. As mentioned previously, the breeding range of the cliff swallow covers nearly all of the continent — except the Deep South of the U.S. and northern Canada. But the birds do not occupy that range uniformly. Their colonies are generally well distanced from one another.

The bird is almost entirely an insect-eater, although it will supplement its diet with a few berries during lean times. For this reason it is not attracted to the feeder. In an area that offers a sheltered vertical surface for nest building, the cliff swallow might be encouraged by the maintenance of a wet, muddy area. Winters in South America.

The cliff swallow lays three to six white eggs spotted with brown. The nest is a grass-, hair- and feather-lined, gourd-shaped structure of mud pellets plastered to the side of a building, bridge, cliff or similar structure.

Spotter's Checklist

Plumage
Steel-blue above, off-white below and forehead, red-brown throat and cheeks, buff underside.

Bill
Short, rounded, black.

Feet
Anisodactyl, dark gray.

Body length
About 5½ inches (14cm).

Size

Habitat
Open agricultural and canyon areas; also along waterways.

Food
Insects and spiders; some berries. Not a feeder bird.

Song
Non-stop twittering and chattering, interspersed with squeaks.

Violet-green swallow

Tachycineta thalassina

The violet-green swallow lays four to five white eggs in a nest of grass and feathers in a cavity in a tree, or some similar opening.

THE VIOLET-green swallow resides in nearly any open habitat, from city skylines to remote canyons to oceanside beaches, throughout its range in the west. It appears to be much less dependent upon water than most other swallow species and therefore occupies a much greater range of habitat. This characteristic also allows the violet-green swallow and other swallow species to live within the same territory without severe competition. It has the same feeding habits as all members of its family, taking only insects that are snatched up while in flight. Large numbers of violet-green swallows have been seen "hawking" for insects over large open areas.

Nest boxes placed in open areas are the only means available to the backyard birdwatcher who would attract this species. Several boxes can be placed close together because the violet-green swallow will nest in loose colonies. Those successful in attracting a nesting group will be treated to an unusual sight when the young birds hatch from the eggs: suddenly, birds that have not nested that season for one reason or another will begin helping the parent birds in bringing food to the nestlings.

Breeds from Alaska south throughout western Canada and the U.S. Winters in central America.

Purple martin

Progne subis

THE PURPLE martin is one of our more famous bird. Even those uninitiated into the ranks of the birdwatcher probably can identify the apartment-style martin house on sight. Although they will nest in a wide variety of natural and artificial cavities, the birds show a decided preference for this group-nesting arrangement high atop a pole. Martin aficionados, in turn, often put great effort into offering more elaborate and larger houses to attract greater and greater colonies of the birds. Many do this for the simple enjoyment of the birds, while others are seeking the incredible insect-eating capacity that a colony of purple martins provides. This benefit was recognized long ago by the Native Americans who hung collections of hollowed gourds from poles around their crop areas.

Water is an important criterion in home range selection for this largest of our swallows. Like most others of the family, purple martins prefer to drink and bathe while in flight. Additional habitat factors that will help to attract the birds are crushed egg shells offered on an elevated table feeder, which the birds eat and share during courtship, and large open areas where they can "hawk" their insect meals.

Breeds from central Canada south throughout the U.S., east of the Rockies and along the Pacific Coast. Winters in South America.

The purple martin lays three to eight white eggs in a grass-lined, shallow cup of grass, twigs, bark, leaves and paper, decorated with fresh green leaves. Nests are placed in a wide variety of cavities, forming a colony.

Spotter's Checklist

Plumage
Dark blue, almost black with purplish tint. Female and young dull dark gray above, lighter below.

Bill
Short, rounded, blue-black.

Feet
Anisodactyl, blue-black.

Body length
About 7¾ inches (20cm).

Size

Habitat
Open areas near stands of trees and generally near freshwater lakes and ponds.

Food
Insects. Not a feeder bird.

Song
"Tea-tea-tea;" also a soft warble.

Chimney swift

Chaetura pelagica

Spotter's Checklist

Plumage
Brownish gray throughout; very short tail.

Bill
Very short, pointed, slight downward curve, black.

Feet
Pamprodactyl, black.

Body length
About 5½ inches (14cm).

Size

Habitat
Very diverse.

Food
Insects. Not a feeder bird.

Song
Series of twitters, chips and clicks in a long string.

The chimney swift lays three to six white eggs in a half-plate of twigs. This is cemented together and attached to the side of a chimney, silo or similar structure with the bird's saliva.

THE CHIMNEY swift is one of the fastest flying of our birds. It also is our most "flyingest," spending every moment of daylight on the wing and stopping only at night for roosting. It does nearly everything on the wing, including mating, gathering nesting material, feeding and drinking. Some have even suggested that the bird sleeps while in flight, although this is questionable.

The chimney swift takes its name from its penchant for roosting and nesting in upright cavities, such as chimneys, lofts, silos and the like. Inside these structures the birds cling to the walls with their feet rather than perching like most other roosting birds. They attach their stick-nests, held together with their own saliva, in the corners or in recesses in the walls. At times large numbers of the birds are seen gathering above such a structure in a growing funnel that suddenly disappears downward into the chimney, silo or whatever.

Appropriate roosting and nesting structures are the only means for attracting this insect-eating species. Large, hollow trees with skyward openings also have been known to be used by colonies of the birds.

Breeds throughout the eastern half of the U.S. and southern Canada. Winters in South America.

Eastern kingbird

Tyrannus tyrannus

THE MEDIUM-sized eastern kingbird takes its name from its aggressive behavior toward other birds, including much larger species such as crows. So relentless is the bird's attack on these trespassers in its territory, which the kingbird tends to define in much larger terms than most species, that the encounter usually continues until the other bird departs. The attack is particularly agitated when the kingbird has its nest in the area. Often an attack on a predator, such as a hawk, will be joined by other small birds in the area. They will mob the bigger bird, swooping and fluttering about it, until it gets their message and flees. After a successful defense of its territory, the kingbird returns to its elevated surveillance perch and issues a victory song of stuttering notes. This same perch is generally used as the launching spot for the "hawking" of insects on the wing, which are snatched, brought back to the perch and eaten there.

Backyards, particularly those that provide open areas, healthy insect populations and ready sources of water are naturally attractive to the kingbird. Nesting might be encouraged with the offering of short bits of string and small, downy feathers, which the bird incorporates into its nest.

Breeds from central Canada south throughout the U.S., except for Pacific Coast and southwestern U.S.

The eastern kingbird lays three to five creamy white eggs spotted with brown and black. The nest is a grass- and plant down-lined cup made of grass, moss and weed stalks with a rough exterior, usually placed on a tree limb anywhere from 2 to 50 feet (0.6-15.2m) off the ground, often over water.

Spotter's Checklist

Plumage
Dark gray above, even darker on head and tail, white below and at tip of tail. Red patch on crown is usually hidden.

Bill
Large, pointed, slight hook on upper mandible, black.

Feet
Anisodactyl, black.

Body length
About 8½ inches (22cm).

Size

Habitat
Open areas, generally near water.

Food
Insects; some berries. Not a feeder bird.

Song
"Dit-zee, dit-zee, dit-zee," with an almost electrical tone.

Least flycatcher

Empidonax minimus

Spotter's Checklist

Plumage
Greenish gray above, white below, white wing bars and eyerings.

Bill
Large, stout, pointed, black over orange.

Feet
Anisodactyl, black.

Body length
About 5¼ inches (13cm).

Size

Habitat
Open areas with mature trees.

Food
Exclusively insects and spiders. Not a feeder bird.

Song
Almost non-stop "chi-beck, chi-beck, chi-beck."

THE LEAST flycatcher is remarkably tame. On the nest it will allow such close approach that it can be touched and even lifted, although this should never be done to any nesting bird. When in pursuit of flying insects it will dive within inches of a human if that is where its prey is. This smallest and most common of our flycatchers prefers a habitat that combines open areas for feeding on insects with stands of large, mature, deciduous trees for nesting and roosting. Nothing else is available to the backyard birdwatcher who would attract the species. However, as with all insect-eating birds, extensive plantings of flowers — particularly native species — without accompanying pesticide use, will encourage healthy insect populations that will in turn attract the birds.

Breeds from central Canada south through northcentral and northeastern U.S. and through the Appalachians. Winters south of the U.S.-Mexican border.

The least flycatcher lays three to six white eggs in a deep cup tightly woven from weed stems, grass and strips of bark. It is lined with plant down, feathers and hair, and usually placed in the fork of a tree or attached to a branch from 2 to 50 feet (0.6-15.2m) off the ground.

Eastern phoebe

Sayornis phoebe

The eastern phoebe lays three to six white eggs; some in each clutch are lightly spotted with brown. The nest is a large, grass- and hair-lined bowl woven from weeds, grasses and mud, and covered with bits of moss. It is usually placed on some shelflike structure, such as a rocky ledge or rafter in a barn, or fixed to the side of a wall or rock face.

THE EASTERN phoebe, one of the tamest birds when on the nest, is believed to have been the first bird species ever banded. Audubon attached a silver thread wire to one leg of several "loose enough so as not to hurt" in 1840 and recorded their return the following spring to the same nest site. The species nested in rock cliffs before European settlers spread across North America, but quickly adapted to the new environment. Human constructions, such as bridge supports and farm buildings are favored today. The vast areas of open grasslands and agricultural fields that accompanied the coming of settlement also are quite conducive to spreading populations of this insect-eater. Because the species destroys no agricultural or garden crops, it is welcomed by nearly everyone for its insect-destroying abilities.

Most of the population migrates to the south in late fall, but some birds remain as far north as New England through the winter. These may supplement their diet with a few berries when the insect supply is limited. It is not a feeder bird, but often will make use of a nesting platform in an area with an ample insect population.

Breeds from central Canada south through the U.S., south to the northern extent of the Deep South, east of the Rockies. Winters as far north as New England.

Spotter's Checklist

Plumage
Brownish green-gray with some white and black lines on wings, off-white below.

Bill
Stout, rounded, black.

Feet
Anisodactyl, black.

Body length
About 7 inches (18cm).

Size

Habitat
Open, wooded areas, generally near water.

Food
Mostly insects and spiders; berries during extreme periods. Not a feeder bird.

Song
"Fee-bee, fee-bee."

Loggerhead shrike

Lanius lodovicianus

Spotter's Checklist

Plumage
Gray crown, neck, back and shoulders; black wings and tail with small amount of white; black mask; white chin, breast and underside.

Bill
Long, pointed, downward curve, black.

Feet
Anisodactyl, black.

Body length
About 9 inches (23cm).

Size

Habitat
Open areas with scattered shrubs.

Food
Larger insects, small mammals and birds and their young. Not a feeder bird.

Song
A variety of twitters and musical notes.

THE LOGGERHEAD shrike is sometimes considered bloodthirsty for its unique method of feeding. Its diet is made up completely of animal life, from large insects to small birds and mammals. It generally dives upon its prey, like some miniature hawk but with its head cocked to deliver a killing or stunning blow with its bill. But because it lacks the talons to grasp its prey for tearing apart, the shrike impales the unlucky creature on the barb of a barbed-wire fence or a large thorn. With its prey thus held in place, it either rips it apart immediately or leaves it there for some future meal. This behavior has earned the loggerhead shrike the nickname of "butcher bird."

Feeders and nesting boxes will not attract this species, but open areas with healthy prey populations adjacent to thorny shrubs, such as hawthorn or bayberry, provide ideal habitat. When you begin to find small creatures impaled on the thorns, you know a shrike has accepted the area. Although there are 67 shrike species worldwide, only the loggerhead and its close cousin the northern shrike are found in North America. The habits of the two species are quite similar, although the loggerhead tends to rely much more on insects for its food.

Breeds from southern Canada south throughout the U.S. Winters as far north as northern California and Virginia.

The loggerhead shrike lays four to six off-white to grayish eggs spotted with brown and gray. The bulky nest is woven from sticks, bark strips weed stems and grasses, and lined with feathers, down and bark strips. It is usually placed in thickly foliaged trees and shrubs from 5 to 30 feet (1.5-9m) off the ground.

Northern flicker
Colaptes auratus

IN SLIGHTLY older books about birds you'll find the northern flicker also referred to as the common flicker, yellow-shafted flicker, red-shafted flicker and gilded flicker. While the first alternative name is simply that, another common name for the bird, the last three are actually races of the overall species: yellow-shafted in the east, red-shafted in the west and gilded in the southwest. The three were considered separate species until recently, when it was verified that they have interbred.

The northern flicker is actually a woodpecker that has widely varied typical woodpecker behavior. The nest is placed in the cavity of a tree, like all other woodpeckers, but the flicker drops to the ground when it comes to feeding. A wide range of insects, nuts, seeds and berries make up their diet, but everything else will be passed by when the chance to feed on ants presents itself. This variation on typical woodpecker behavior has equipped the flicker to adapt more easily to change, and residential areas, parks and agricultural areas with limited mature trees will support this bird just fine. Although the species is not generally a feeder bird; nest boxes will be used.

Breeds continentwide except for northern Alaska and Canada. Winters throughout the U.S. and north throughout Canada along the Pacific Coast.

The northern flicker lays three to ten white eggs in the wood chips that have fallen into a hole dug by both parent birds in a tree, utility pole or fencepost. The entrance to the hole might be anywhere from 2 to 60 feet (0.6-18.2m) off the ground.

Spotter's Checklist

Plumage
Gray-brown back, wings and tail with many black spots; white breast and underside with many black spots and large black band at base of neck; blue-gray cap and back of neck with bright red patch; buff face with black band from bill to lower cheeks.

Bill
Long, pointed, gray.

Feet
Zygodactyl, gray.

Body length
About 12 inches (30cm).

Size

Habitat
Open wooded areas; also wooded desert areas.

Food
Ants, other insects and berries. Visit feeders only during severe periods; when they do, they come to suet and sunflower seeds.

Song
"Wick-a, wick-a, wick-a."

Downy woodpecker

Picoides pubescens

The downy woodpecker lays three to six white eggs in a hole that the parents dig in a tree, stump or fencepost. The entrance hole is between 3 and 50 feet (1-15.2m) off the ground.

THE DOWNY woodpecker is the most common woodpecker across much of the continent. In general, only large expanses of treeless terrain, such as in the southwestern U.S. will lack a population of the bird. It's also the smallest and least wary of humans. When approached on the side of a tree, the bird's reaction generally will be simply to hop to the other side. Any backyard feeder within its range that offers suet will attract the species on a daily schedule. The downy woodpecker is often seen among the mixed flocks of small birds that roam woodlands and backyards in the winter, including chickadees, creepers, kinglets, nuthatches and other small woodpecker species.

In addition to their spring mating courtship rituals, downy woodpeckers enter a brief period of courtshiplike behavior each fall. Both sexes display in front of each other and clash in flight with others of the same sex. In both spring and fall territorial displays, the woodpeckers drum on the sides of trees in lieu of song. Within a few days the urge seems to pass and the birds separate, each individual finding its own tree into which it will drill its winter roosting hole. The hairy woodpecker is nearly identical to the downy woodpecker, although the former is about 50 percent larger.

Resident continentwide except for northern Canada and southwestern U.S.

Pileated woodpecker
Dryocopus pileatus

The pileated woodpecker lays three to five white eggs in a conical hole that the parents excavate in a tree. The entrance hole is between 15 to 70 feet (4.5-21.3m) off the ground.

HISTORICALLY THE pileated woodpecker is a resident of the deep woods, but in the past few decades it has demonstrated a surprising ability to adapt to change. The species has now become abundant at the edges of towns and even cities. This is in marked contrast to the early twentieth century, when the species was rare throughout its former range in the east. The reason for the species' resurgence has been the abandonment of farmlands and their rebirth into second-growth forests, and the development of woodlandlike suburbs.

The pileated woodpecker is a large bird with a brightly colored head and white-splashed black wings that can extend to 30 inches (76cm) tip-to-tip, but it is often difficult to spot as it works among the uppermost lengths of tree trunks. Its presence is more often discerned by its loud call and its thunderous drilling on the sides of trees.

The work of the species is easy to detect. The tree will be honeycombed with rectangular holes three or four inches (7-10cm) wide and chips will cover the ground. The object is often a colony of carpenter ants. Some trees have actually been saved by the bird's attack on the ants, which would otherwise have killed them.

Resident throughout central Canada south through the Rockies, along the West Coast and throughout the eastern U.S.

Red-headed woodpecker
Melanerpes erythrocephalus

Spotter's Checklist

Plumage
Red head and neck; black back, shoulders and wings with large white patches on wings; white breast and underside.

Bill
Large, stout, pointed, white with black at tip.

Feet
Zygodactyl, off-white.

Body length
About 10 inches (25cm).

Size

Habitat
Open wooded areas.

Food
Insects, nuts, berries and fruits. At the feeder, suet, peanut butter, whole peanuts, nuts, oil-type sunflower seeds.

Song
"Queer, queer, queer," rather grating.

THE RED-headed woodpecker has been a species in decline for several decades primarily for two reasons: the European starling competes aggressively and successfully against it for nesting cavities, and humans tend to remove the dead and dying trees that would provide more of such cavities. However, the species is still common throughout the eastern half of the U.S. and southern Canada. Open agricultural and residential areas with stands of mature trees, some of which are dead or dying, are prime habitat for the red-headed woodpecker.

Despite its loss to the European starling, the red-headed woodpecker is usually the dominant woodpecker species within its territory. It actively drives other woodpeckers from that territory, either because it is nesting at the time or to protect the scattered stashes of nuts, seeds and berries that it has squirreled away for winter use. The red-headed woodpecker is an active food-storer, filling a large proportion of the crevices and crannies within its territory through the course of the fall. It adopts the same territorial attitudes towards a backyard with a feeder that provides favored food items, notably large seeds and nuts. Regular visits can be observed throughout the day.

Winters in South America.

The red-headed woodpecker lays four to seven white eggs in a hole that the parents excavate in a tree, snag, utility pole or fencepost. The entrance hole is anywhere between 8 and 80 feet (2.5-24.3m) off the ground.

Red-bellied woodpecker
Melanerpes carolinus

THE RED-bellied woodpecker is a common species across the southeastern United States but less numerous into the northern extent of its range, which reaches to the U.S.-Canadian border at the Great Lakes. However it's more common in this northern area than it was previously, largely because of its ability to adapt readily to life in towns and cities. A telephone pole or a backyard tree have proved to be as acceptable for drilling a nest cavity as a tree in the deep woodlands. Similarly, the red-bellied woodpecker is readily attracted to feeders, particularly those where suet or pieces of orange are offered. The natural foods of the bird are insects and nuts.

The bird feeds in normal woodpecker-fashion on the sides of trees, but also spends a large amount of time on the ground foraging through leaf litter. It is one of the woodpecker species that habitually stores large quantities of nuts and seeds through the fall for later use in the winter. The species will use nesting boxes, but it prefers natural cavities and those that it carves into dead and dying trees. Because of its black-and-white striped back, the bird is sometimes known as the zebraback.

Resident throughout eastern U.S. as far west as Texas, except for New England states.

The red-bellied woodpecker lays three to eight white eggs in a hole in a tree, stump, utility pole or fencepost. The entrance hole is usually from 5 to 40 feet (1.5-12m) off the ground.

Black-chinned hummingbird

Archilochus alexandri

Spotter's Checklist

Plumage
Bright green above, white below with areas of greenish tint, black throat with iridescent border of purple.

Bill
Very long, pointed, slight downward curve, black.

Feet
Anisodactyl, black.

Body length
About 3¾ inches (9cm).

Size

Habitat
Widespread.

Food
Flower nectar, small insects. At the feeder, sugar water.

Song
Very high-pitched and shrill chattering.

The black-chinned hummingbird lays two white eggs in a cup of plant fibers, wool and lichens held together with insect silk on the branch of a shrub or small tree.

THE BLACK-chinned hummingbird is the most song-prone of our hummingbirds, regularly issuing its high-pitched song that sounds quite a bit like a human whistling through teeth. The male bird also offers a remarkable courtship flight, flying several figure-eights in view of his mate. After his interest in mating has passed, he will move to a new territory where he finds an ample supply of insects and nectar-producing, tubular flowers. When the season for both these sources of food passes, both sexes migrate to the south. The entire population winters south of the U.S.-Mexican border.

Hummingbird feeders will attract the species, but the birds are often so numerous that larger feeding containers, such as poultry waterers, may be a worthwhile investment. More than a hundred black-chinned hummingbirds have been counted in a single backyard equipped with ample feeders and flower beds. Mature, flowering tree tobacco will also draw large numbers. The bird is historically a resident of the dry, scrub areas throughout the west, but it has found the backyards of suburbia to its liking as well.

Breeds from southwesternmost Canada south throughout the western U.S. as far east as Texas.

Ruby-throated hummingbird

Archilochus colubris

The ruby-throated hummingbird lays two white eggs in a plant down-lined cup made of coarser down, plant fibers and bits of buds, covered on the outside with lichens. The nest is attached to a downward-slanting tree branch with spider silk, 6 to 50 feet (1.8-15.2m) off the ground. It is usually sheltered by overhanging leaves.

IF YOU see a hummingbird east of the Mississippi River, chances are very heavily weighted in favor of it being a ruby-throated hummingbird. The species is the only hummingbird that naturally resides in this region, although sometimes the occasional western species does stray eastward. The entire population of the ruby-throated hummingbird winters as far north as the U.S. Gulf Coast in mild winters, but more commonly south of the U.S.-Mexican border. However, large numbers of the birds return to the eastern United States and southeastern Canada in early spring, well before most flower species are in bloom to provide the birds with nectar.

Insects make up a certain portion of the species' diet, but the real source of the species' ability to survive before large numbers of flowers are available lies with the yellow-bellied sapsucker. It seems the hummingbird follows these tree-drillers about during the early spring in the northern woodlands, sharing in the sap that builds up in the wells that the sapsuckers drill in tree trunks and the insects that gather there.

Hummingbird feeders will attract good numbers of these birds, as will plantings of tubular flowers. In both instances, the color red definitely enhances the attraction. However, with the welfare of the birds in mind, choose feeders with red-colored materials in their construction or tie red ribbons about them, rather than adding food dye to the sugar-water solution in the feeders.

Breeds throughout southern Canada and U.S., east of the Mississippi.

Spotter's Checklist

Plumage
Metallic green above, lighter below, bright red chin and throat. Female lacks red.

Bill
Long, needlelike, black.

Feet
Anisodactyl, black.

Body length
About 3½ inches (9cm).

Size

Habitat
Open, wooded areas.

Food
Flower nectar, tree sap and some insects. At the feeder, sugar water.

Song
A squeaking twitter, a great deal like the squeak of a mouse.

Anna's hummingbird
Calypte anna

THE ANNA'S hummingbird is one of two hummers named in the early nineteenth century for the Duke and Duchess of Rivoli in France. Anna's was named for the Duchess, while Rivoli's was named for the Duke. The species is primarily a resident of the West Coast of the United States, but the spread of hummingbird feeders and the planting of eucalyptus trees and fuchsias have helped the species to expand its territory both inland and to the north, as far as British Columbia. It is the only hummingbird species that winters in significant numbers within the United States.

Anna's hummingbird is at home both in populated and uninhabited areas, where the male treats observers to a spectacular courtship flight. Climbing high into the air, he suddenly turns and dives toward the branch where the female is perched in a series of circles. As he pulls up, at the conclusion of his dive, he utters what can best be described as a bark. The tiny bird is a vigorous defender of its territory, although spreading juveniles of the year in late summer generally overwhelm the adult birds and crowd their territories. At this time, good numbers of the species may be attracted.

The Anna's hummingbird lays two white eggs in a cup woven from twigs and lichen, and attached to the branch of a small tree or shrub. The nest is usually sheltered by an overhanging branch.

142

Ring-necked pheasant

Phasianus colchicus

RING-NECKED pheasants won't be found in every backyard within their range throughout the northeastern, mid-western and (scattered) western United States and southcentral Canada. As a matter of fact, it won't be found in nearly as many backyards across that range as it was just 20 years ago. The bird's population has been on a sharp downward spiral since the mid-1970s, largely because of habitat loss and changing agricultural practices. If you live in a housing development look out of any window and you'll see the first. And, if you live near farming areas watch how early hayfields are mown in the summer and you'll witness the other: the destruction of nests, chicks and adults on the nest in the blades of the mower. In many states of the Northeast, huntable populations of the popular gamebird are maintained only through the introduction each fall, and to a lesser extent each spring, of game-farm-raised birds. The central plains population has fared better.

The ring-necked pheasant is not a native species. It was introduced here from Asia in 1887. The fact that it has since become America's premier gamebird speaks well of how adaptable and successful the bird has been in its new home, at least until our modern ways came into conflict with it. Backyards that border on weedy areas, such as pastures, can still readily attract small flocks of the bird with the offering of corn on the ground, or better yet under low-hanging conifer branches.

The ring-necked pheasant lays six to 16 greenish to pinkish brown eggs in a shallow scrape on the ground, lined with weeds, grass and leaves.

Spotter's Checklist

Plumage
Patterned in various shades of brown scattered with black and dark brown spots and chevrons of white; reddish brown at breast and flanks; white neck ring; blue- or green-tinted head with bright red at eye; tail as long as or longer than body. Female is mottled, but generally lighter brown throughout, with a much shorter tail.

Bill
Short, stout, rounded, yellow.

Feet
Anisodactyl, greenish tan.

Body length
About 34 inches (86cm).

Size

Habitat
Weedy agricultural areas, pastures and meadows, swamps.

Food
Large seeds, grains, fruits, berries, insects and spiders. At the feeder, corn.

Song
A very loud, double-phrase cackle, repeated several times with intervals between.

Northern bobwhite

Colinus virginianus

THE NORTHERN bobwhite is another popular gamebird that must be considered in any thorough treatment of backyard birds of North America. Unlike the pheasant, it's a native species. Its numbers today are definitely greater than before the dense woodlands east of the Mississippi River were opened up, but not nearly so great as they were in the first half of the century. Like the pheasant, the bobwhite's population has experienced the effects of the double-edged sword of habitat loss and changing agricultural practices. In the bobwhite's situation however, the most devastating change has been the loss of weedy and brushy borders and pasturelands.

The loss of this bird is most notable in the northern extent of its range, where the wonderful "bob-WHITE" call now is a rarity. To the south the bird still exists in appreciable numbers, and each summer after the nesting season, birds gather into coveys of one or two dozen birds each. The covey is a defensive mechanism, allowing the birds to maintain surveillance in all directions and to blast off in all directions when threatened, thereby startling a would-be predator. After such an explosion, individual birds begin their familiar calling to draw the covey back together.

Resident throughout eastern U.S. as far north as Great Lakes; also elsewhere as introduced by humans.

The northern bobwhite lays 10 to 20 off-white eggs in a grass- and weed-lined hollow in a clump of grass or weeds on the ground, often with an arch of weeds woven above the nest.

California quail
Callipela californica

Throughout its range from British Columbia south through the West Coast states, the California quail occurs in eight different races. Humans have served to confuse the issue even further by introducing the gamebird species into areas far east of its normal range and destroying its traditional habitat. Valley floors, the slopes of oak foothills and chaparral areas of the uplands are all used by the bird, which is rather public in its behavior. Like most of its close relatives it tends to roost in small trees and shrubs rather than on the ground, but it feeds in open areas rather than the brushy spots chosen by most of its brethren. In courtship, the male tends to leap up into a tree or onto a fence post to cackle out its territorial claim.

Grit is a prime attraction for the California quail, which is often seen picking that substance along the sides of roadways. It will also come to ground feeders for cracked corn and millet. In the wild its food is primarily made up of filaree, turkey mullein, barley, clover, lupine, deervetch, oak, thistle and pigweed. Mature plantings of these species will draw in any quail in the area.

The California quail lays 10 to 15 light brown eggs spotted with darker brown in a grass-lined depression on the ground.

Spotter's Checklist

Plumage
Chocolate brown on back, white flecks on sides, scaled golden tan underside, gray breast, black face with white outline, chestnut crown, dark brown head plume.

Bill
Short, conical, sharp, black.

Feet
Anisodactyl, black.

Body length
About 10 inches (25cm).

Size

Habitat
Brushy, weedy areas; open wooded areas with thick understory.

Food
Plant leaves in spring; seeds at other times. At the feeder, cracked corn, oil-type sunflower seeds, grains.

Song
"Shhh-ca-cow;" also a low clucking while feeding.

Rock dove (Pigeon)
Columbia livia

BETTER KNOWN as the domestic pigeon, or less affectionately as the "rat with wings," the rock dove is a common species nearly everywhere in the United States and southern Canada, except heavily wooded regions. So prolific are the birds that large-scale efforts at eradicating them in city after city from coast to coast have failed miserably. The rock dove just might be one of those species, with the cockroach, house rat, feral cats and dogs, and coyotes, that could remain in possession of the Earth long after humanity's time here has concluded. The species has been introduced successfully in cities nearly worldwide.

Populations of the species were much less common before the huge woodlands that once dominated much of North America were opened up. However, residential and agricultural areas have proven agreeable to the rock dove, which can make a meal of nearly everything organic found there from popcorn offered by well-meaning people to garbage and litter. Many variations of the basic rock dove have been bred, and the bird even has its legion of enthusiasts. In the backyard, it will come to any offering on the ground or elevated feeding tables.

The rock dove lays one or two white eggs on a very loose platform of grass, sticks and litter on a ledge or in a cranny.

Mourning dove

Zenaida macroura

LIKE THE pigeon, the mourning dove has been a major beneficiary of the European settlement of North America. The species' population today is probably hundreds of times what it was historically. Also, like the pigeon, nearly everything offered at the backyard feeder will attract the species. Cracked corn is favored. Bird baths hold a particular fascination and small flocks will spend considerable time at these locations.

In some states the mourning dove is officially considered a songbird and no hunting of the species is permitted. In these states incredible flocks of the birds can be seen mobbing feeders and quickly depleting all food offered to other species.

In other states the bird is a gamebird and its population is kept at more reasonable levels, but even here the species can build to fantastic numbers. Some surveys of backyard birdwatchers have come up with numbers as high as 75-80 percent for the proportion of backyard feeders that have at least some mourning doves coming to them. In general, the bird is welcomed in the backyard, except where its numbers are out of control, and it rewards the bird-watcher with the lovely call from which it takes its name.

Breeds throughout the U.S. and southern Canada. Winters as far north as the U.S.-Canadian border.

The mourning dove lays two to four (most often two) white eggs on a loosely woven platform of sticks. It is sometimes lined with grass and weeds. The nest is usually placed in the crook of a tree or shrub anywhere from 8 to 50 feet (2.5-15.2m) off the ground.

Spotter's Checklist

Plumage
Buff-gray with a pinkish tint on breast and underside; black spots on lower wings.

Bill
Short, sharp, gray.

Feet
Anisodactyl, reddish.

Body length
About 12 inches (30cm).

Size

Habitat
Very widespread, generally in weedy or grassy areas with mature trees.

Food
Seeds, grains. At the feeder, cracked corn, sunflower seeds.

Song
"Cooooo, cooooo," with a twirling, rolling quality; one or both notes may also slur into "cooo-ah."

Spotter's Checklist

Plumage
Brownish gray with scaled blue-gray head, neck, breast and underside; reddish brown tint and black spots on wings.

Bill
Short, pointed, red-orange.

Feet
Anisodactyl, gray.

Body length
About 6½ inches (16cm).

Size

Habitat
Weedy agricultural and rangeland areas.

Food
Seeds, plant parts, some insects. At the feeder, grains.

Song
"Cooooo, cooooo;" one or both may slur into "coo-ah."

Common ground dove
Columbina passerina

THE COMMON ground dove occupies a much smaller range than either of the other species presented on the previous pages, and within that range it tends to occur sporadically in one locale but not another. In recent years, however, the species, resident from the southern U.S. south, seems to be extending both its range to the north and its residence within its range. Both extensions have been slow in emerging as trends.

It's a much shyer bird than most doves, keeping mostly to weedy, brushy cover. However it can be drawn into the backyard if such cover is provided. Seeds and grains spread in such locations will add to the attraction. Mature fencerow-type plantings are a favored habitat for the species, and bird baths are very effective in attracting them. Outside the breeding season, ground doves travel in small flocks. For nesting they pair off and go their separate ways.

The common ground dove lays two or three off-white eggs in a loose cup of plant fibers and rootlets. This may be placed on the ground or to as high as 10 feet (3m) off the ground in many different types of trees, shrubs, cacti and vines.

Barn owl
Tyto alba

Spotter's Checklist

Plumage
Soft buff-brown above with gray and white patches and black and white spots; heart-shaped white face framed in buff-brown; white underside with spots.

Bill
Short, stout, hooked downward, white.

Feet
Zygodactyl, off-white to gray.

Body length
About 18 inches (46cm).

Size

Habitat
Open agricultural and residential areas, generally near human dwellings.

Food
Small rodents. Not a feeder bird.

Song
Succession of hisses, screams, clicks and grunts, accompanied with snapping of the bill.

UNINHABITED BUILDINGS, are favored roosting and nesting sites of the barn owl. Its common name, of course, has been derived from this behavior. The bird is at home in close proximity to humans and finds our barnyards, vacant city lots and garbage dumps teaming with the rodents that make up its diet.

The barn owl has been the most successful of all North American owl species in adapting to the changes that we have brought to the natural landscape. It hunts mostly at night and may go largely undetected except for its strange, clicking, hissing, screaming call. Although the barn owl has excellent night-vision, much of its hunting is done with its exceptional hearing.

The species remains common from year to year throughout the southern half of its range, but to the north it tends to swing between periods when there are many and periods when there are practically none. As with many predators, these swings are tied to ups and downs in the prey population. The species tends to nest in response to these same prey populations and active nests have been found in every month of the year. Nest boxes are the backyard birdwatcher's primary means of attracting the bird.

Resident from southern Canada south throughout U.S.

The barn owl lays three to 12 off-white eggs in a cavity or on a level surface in a wide range of structures from barns to caves. The owl builds no nest, but the nesting area may appear as if it does because it is usually coated with owl pellets.

Eastern screech owl
Otus asio

Spotter's Checklist

Plumage
Mottled red-brown to gray with patches of white and black; ear tufts.

Bill
Short, hooked downward, hidden by feathers of face.

Feet
Zygodactyl, gray.

Body length
About 10 inches (25cm).

Size

Habitat
Open wooded areas with mature trees.

Food
Very varied, including larger insects, crustaceans, small rodents and birds. Not a feeder bird.

Song
A horse-like whinny, but softer and with a mournful tone.

THE LITTLE eastern screech owl is by far the commonest owl species of the eastern half of the United States. They have adapted to the human environment and are equally at home in suburbia and deep woodland. The species exhibits two distinct color phases, gray and red, which are linked to none of the normal criteria that would account for this: not sex, not age, not season. As a matter of fact, a single brood of nestlings may very well include some of the "normal" gray phase and some of the red phase. An intermediate brown phase has also been documented. The color variations are the result of extra red pigment in the plumage of the red-phase birds.

While the screech owl has been known to take prey as large as rats and pigeons, its diet more commonly includes a wide array of smaller creatures. They eat a greater proportion of insects than do the large owl species. The eastern screech owl will also take small fish and crayfish from streams. It is a night-hunter, relying on its powerful hearing ability to locate and capture its prey. What appear to be its ears on superficial observation are really nothing more than tufts of feathers where one might expect to find ears. The owl's real ears are actually on the sides of its head.

Resident throughout U.S. and southwestern Canada.

The screech owl lays two to seven white eggs in many types of cavities, including the abandoned holes of other species, on whatever debris or litter is already there. That debris can also come to include owl feathers and fur or feathers from prey species.

American kestrel
Falco sparverius

EVEN THE most ardent haters of birds of prey, such as small-game hunters, generally have no squabble with the American kestrel. The smallest and most common falcon on the continent, its prey is primarily insects, although it regularly takes small birds, mammals, reptiles and amphibians — hence one of the common nicknames for the species: sparrow hawk. House sparrows are in fact a chief prey species for those kestrels that live within our cities.

Under legal protection and with the opening of vast woodlands into grassy, weedy areas, the population of American kestrels has exploded in recent years. Today it is difficult to locate any open country that doesn't have its kestrel perched on a power line. The northern populations mostly migrate south of the U.S.-Canadian border for the winter, but south of the border many birds are year-round residents. Except for a brief period in late summer, when adult birds may be seen with their new families; the American kestrel is generally a solitary figure. Even during the mating and nesting period, the female tends to remain on the nest while the male brings food to her, and later to her and the nestlings.

Breeds from Alaska and central Canada south throughout the U.S. Winters from British Columbia and Connecticut south.

The American kestrel lays three to five off-white to tan eggs sparsely spotted with brown, often at one end of the egg, in a tree cavity, a cranny in a building or the abandoned hole of another species. Little if any nesting material is used.

Spotter's Checklist

Plumage
Red-tan with blue-gray shoulders, wings and crown; white cheeks, chin and flanks; black-tipped wings and tail; vertical black earlines and eyelines; black spots throughout.

Bill
Short, stout, hooked downward, yellow near face, metallic gray beyond.

Feet
Anisodactyl, yellow.

Body length
About 10 inches (25cm).

Size

Habitat
Open grassy and weedy areas.

Food
Mostly insects, but also small mammals, birds and reptiles. Not a feeder bird.

Song
"Killy-killy-killy," swift and shrill.

Red-tailed hawk

Buteo jamaicensis

Spotter's Checklist

Plumage
Mottled shades of brown with some patches of off-white, a variable band of dark brown across the belly, and a red-brown tail. Young are duller and without red-brown tail.

Bill
Large, broad, hooked downward, gray near face, black tip.

Feet
Anisodactyl, dull grayish yellow.

Body length
About 23 inches (58cm).

Size

Habitat
Open wooded and agricultural areas.

Food
Rodents, reptiles, rabbits. Not a feeder bird.

Song
"Keeeeeeeee-errrrrr," slurred and descending.

THE RED-tailed hawk is the most common larger hawk in North America. This is the species regularly seen soaring over farmlands or perched in trees at the edge of such areas. It is able to make use of a wide range of habitats, from the smallest of woodland stands in the east to canyon cliffs in the west to cacti lands in the southwest. The only real limitation on a local population is the number of rodents. Any animal from mice to rabbits is prey for the species, which also takes the occasional snake. Disappearing agricultural areas may be reducing the bird's population in the east.

Although it is primarily a predator it is not at all above scavenging on carcasses, such as road-kills. The red-tailed hawk is also North America's most varied hawk in terms of plumage. The variation occurs with geographic differences. Most adults can be identified by their red tails, but even this is not constant. A western race of dark-brown birds was previously considered a separate species, known as Harlan's hawk. The red-tailed hawk is not readily attracted to the feeder, but it will feed on other birds and animals attracted there.

Breeds from Alaska and northern Canada south throughout the U.S. Winters throughout U.S. and north into Canada along the two coasts.

The red-tailed hawk lays one to five off-white to blue-white eggs (often blotched) in a vine bark-, moss- and evergreen twig-lined cup. This is placed at the center of a shallow but well-made platform of sticks. The nest is usually placed in a tree from 35 to 80 feet (10.7-24.3m) off the ground.

Killdeer
Charadrius vociferus

THE KILLDEER is one of those birds with so distinctive a call that it was allowed to assign itself a name. It's a common sight along our shores, on farmlands, on golf courses, on stone-covered parking lots and similar areas. For nesting, it prefers gravel areas within those large habitat types.

The female makes her nest in a slight depression that she may or may not line with a bit of grass. She relies on the camouflage coloring of the eggs and chicks and on her ability to distract intruders to protect the next generation. When her nest is approached, the female gives an Oscar-worthy performance. Suddenly she is severely injured. Trailing a wing she moves weakly away from the nest. When the predator takes the bait and goes for her, the female suddenly recovers and flies off leaving the predator with nothing more than the echo of her call.

In general the killdeer will respond to nothing that the backyard birdwatcher may do to attempt to attract it. Its diet is entirely insect- and crustacean-based. Water is an attraction, but the bird can usually find enough to satisfy its needs in a wet field.

Breeds from central Canada south throughout the U.S. Winters as far north as New Jersey and along Pacific Coast.

The killdeer lays three to five light brown eggs heavily spotted and scrawled with black and dark brown in a depression on the ground, usually with a wide view of its surroundings. The depression may be lined with grass, small stones and other litter.

Mallard
Anas platyrhynchos

Spotter's Checklist

Plumage
Gray to near-silver overall, darker along back and tail; white at tail; thin white neck ring; emerald green head and neck; brownish breast. Female mottled brown, blue speculum, white tail.

Bill
Long, flat, rounded. Male greenish yellow with black tip. Female mottled brown and orange.

Feet
Palmate, orange.

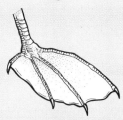

Body length
About 24 inches (61 cm).

Size

Habitat
Waterways of all sorts.

Food
Vegetation. At the feeder, grains and cracked corn, if near water.

Song
Various quacks, both loud and soft.

THE MALLARD really cannot be considered a backyard species, except in those backyards that have substantial areas of open water. A mini-pond or bird bath does not qualify. However, wherever such open water does occur, from city park to woodland pothole, the mallard will likely be found. It is the most readily identified waterfowl species in North America.

Where the mallard occurs it is relatively unconcerned about being in close proximity to humans, even to the point of being "trained" to accept food from the hand, and to show up at a given location at about the same time each day for feeding. Backyards that are located with an unobstructed path to open water — no roadways or parking lots between the two points — can be visited by "trained" birds, even if the distance between the two points is several hundred feet. A trail of cracked corn from the water to the desired feeding location will quickly educate the birds about the presence of food.

The mallard is the ancestor of our white domestic duck and interbreeding between the two still produces a wide array of plumage patterns. The mallard also interbreeds with some other wild species, notably the black duck.

Breeds throughout the U.S., Alaska and all but northernmost Canada. Winters mostly south of the U.S.-Canadian border.

The mallard lays six to 15 light greenish tan eggs in a depression on the ground, mounded up with grass, reeds and strips of wetland plants. The nest is lined with feathers and down that the female plucks from her own breast.

Canada goose
Branta canadensis

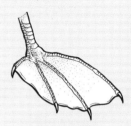

WHAT THE rock dove is to our city streets and parks, the Canada goose is to our parks across much of the continent. The species is extremely tolerant of humans and quick to take advantage of any food source that they offer.

They are famous for their V-shaped flying formations in migration, but incredible numbers of the birds have become year-round residents in our parks, where they frequently become a nuisance species that must be live-trapped and removed to wilder areas.

Except during the nesting period, the Canada goose is a flock bird. Under nearly all circumstances a few members of each flock will be on watch at all times, the various individuals sharing in this duty.

The species is a much sought-after game species for hunters and a major pest species for farmers in some areas. Although the birds are generally not backyard species, they will respond quickly to any offering of cracked or whole corn on properties close to large expanses of open water.

Breeds from Alaska and Baffin Island south into the northern third of the U.S. Winters throughout most of the U.S.

The Canada goose lays four to 10 off-white eggs in a down-lined mound of sticks, grasses and wetland plants either on the ground or on a low stump near or in the water.

Index

Acknowledgements

Quarto would like to thank the following for providing photographs, and for permission to reproduce copyright material. While every effort has been made to trace and acknowledge all copyright holders, we would like to apologize should there have been any omissions.

Key
A = Above
M = Middle
B = Below
AL = Above left
AR = Above right
BL = Below left
BR = Below right

p2 Maslowski Photo. p6 Leonard Lee. p7 Maslowski Photo. p8L Leonard Lee. R, John Gerlach/Visuals Unlimited. p9 M Dixon. p10-13 Maslowski Photo. p14 Leonard Lee. p15A Bill Beatty/Visuals Unlimited. BL, Richard B Dippold/Unicorn Stock Photos. BR, W M Grenfell/Visuals Unlimited. p16L, Maslowski Photo. R, Gay Bumgarner/Photonats inc. p17A, Maslowski Photo. B, Leonard Lee. p18L, John D Cunningham/Visuals Unlimited. R, Leonard Lee. p20, Stephen J Lang/Visuals Unlimited. p21L, Maslowski Photo. R, Leonard Lee. p22L, Maslowski Photo. R, Leonard Lee. p23A, Leonard Lee. BL, Maslowski Photo. BR, M Schneck. p24L, Maslowski/Visuals Unlimited. p25L, Gary Svoboda. R, Maslowski Photo. p26L, Leonard Lee. R, Karl H Maslowski. p27A, S and D Maslowski. B, S. Maslowski/Visuals Unlimited. p29 Maslowski Photo. p30 Leonard Lee. p31 David C Bitters/Photonats inc. p32 Martha McBride/Unicorn Stock Photos. p33 Robert Villani/Visuals Unlimited. p34L, Maslowski Photo. R, Daphne Kinzler/Visuals Unlimited. p35A, Maslowski Photo. B, Martha McBride/Unicorn Stock Photo. p39AL, Maslowski Photo. AR, David M Stone/ Photonats inc. BL and BR, Maslowski Photo. p41AL and AR, Leonard Lee. BL, Bernard Hehl/Unicorn Stock Photos. BR, Bill Beatty/Visuals Unlimited. p42L and M, Maslowski Photo. R, Steve Maslowski. p43 Maslowski Photo/Visuals Unlimited. p44L, Maslowski Photo. R, Len Rue Jr. p45AL, Steve Maslowski. AR, George McCarthy. B, Maslowski Photo. p46 Tom Ulrich/Visuals Unlimited. p47AL, Maslowski Photo. AR, Leonard Lee. B, Don Johnston/Photonats inc. p49AL, Bernard Hehl/Unicorn Stock Photos. AR, Maslowski Photo. BL, William J Webber/Visuals Unlimited. BR, Leonard Lee. p50 Paul Forrester/Quarto. p51L, AnealVohra/Unicorn Stock Photos. R, John Serao/Visuals Unlimited. p52 and 53 Karl and Steve Maslowski.